Family Spirit

The Ifá Concept of Egun

Ifa Theology
volume 2

Family Spirit

The Ifá Concept of Egun

Awo Falokun Fatunmbi
Egbe Ifa Ogunti Ode Remo

Athelia Henrietta Press
Publishing in the Name of Òrúnmìlà

Library of Congress Control Number: 2006924603

ISBN: 1-890157-40-6

Editorial: Roger Francis
Production: Rudolph Francis
Assistant Production: Adesola Osakalumi
Continuity: Patrick Oguntade

Interior and cover design and prep by Mulberry Tree Press, Inc.
Printed and bound in Canada.

Athelia Henrietta Press, Inc.
Publishing In The Name of Òrùnmìlà
1194 Nostrand Avenue, Brooklyn, N.Y. 11225 U.S.A.
Tel. (718) 493-4500 / Fax (718) 467-0099

Email: Atheliahenriettapress@yahoo.com

Contents

Acknowledgements

I THANK THOSE ELDERS who taught me *Awo Egun,* the mystery of ancestor reverence. *Kikan mase Araba* Adesanya Awoyade, who initiated me into the mysteries of *Ifa*.

In terms of making this book possible I want to extend a special thanks to Francis Charteris for her considered suggestions as an editor, and to Esubiyi (www.gallery-esubiyii.com) for his inspired artwork. For her boundless support and inspiration I want to express my profound gratitude to Iyanifa Fasegun Fatunmbi who helped me grasp the importance of Iyanifa and Iyaami as foundations for Ifa. She can be reached at csomina@hotmail.com. To all those who made this book possible I say *a dupe pupo* (many thanks).

Ire
Awo Falokun Fatunmbi
Egbe Ifa Ogunti Ode Remo

Family Spirit

The Ifá Concept of Egun

Introduction

THIS IS THE SECOND VOLUME in a series of books on the theology of *Ifá*, the traditional religion of Yoruba culture. Volume 1 described the *Ifá* concept of *ori* (consciousness). According to *Ifá* oral tradition *ori* is the seat of consciousness and the receptacle of spiritual influences emanating from the Ancestral Realm (*Ọrun*). *Ori* functions in polarity with the physical heart called *Okan* in Yoruba. The *okan* is the seat of all emotions collectively called *ẹgbẹ*. *Ifá* teaches that spiritual growth is the integration of thoughts and emotions; an ongoing process of stabilizing tension between the head and the heart. When *ori* and *ẹgbẹ* are in alignment the individual experiences *ire* meaning good fortune. When *ori* and *ẹgbẹ* are in conflict the individual experiences *ibi* meaning misfortune. *Ifá* is the preservation of the ancestral wisdom that gives guidance on how to maintain balance between the head and the heart as we move through the developmental stages of life. *Ifá* is not a doctrine of belief; it is a way of looking at the world based on the experience of connection to Spirit.

We connect to Spirit through the *ori inu* the inner self, the seat of perception and the unknowable knower. The inner self becomes known to consciousness (*ori*) as the head and heart unit. Access to *ori-inu* facilitates altered states of consciousness commonly described as possession.

Traditional Yoruba culture integrates Spirit communication with personal development to facilitate further spiritual growth. Messages from Spirit can include a vision of the higher self (*ipo̱nri*). The perception of *ipo̱nri* is a vision of human potential or destiny (*ayanmo*). *Ifá* teaches that destiny is based on a personal manifestation of *iwa-pe̱le̱* meaning good character. According to *Ifá* cosmology we are born good and blessed children (*o̱mo̱ rere*) and choose a destiny prior to incarnation that reflects our essential goodness. Finding our destiny involves a desire to do the right thing in any given moment.

Ifá's spiritual legacy predates recorded history. It emerged from a time when the veil between human consciousness and the voice of Spirit was extremely thin. In the words of *Ifá* oral scripture, Yoruba cosmology developed at a time when both humans and Spirits walked the Earth. It is my personal belief that our ancient African ancestors had clear access to inter-dimensional beings (*Oris̱a* and *Egun*) who gave them clear and effective instruction on how to place the head and the heart in alignment, and, in that place of alignment the ancient Yoruba were taught the mystery of living in harmony with the natural environment.

A Yoruba proverb says we become who we are by standing on the shoulders of those who come before us. From the perspective of traditional Yoruba culture, remembering those who came before us is a sacred obligation. Each generation takes responsibility for preserving the wisdom of the ancestors. In most earth-centered cultures, meaning those cultures that make an effort to live in harmony with Nature, dissemination of ancestral wisdom is the foundation of the methodology used to guide consciousness along the path leading from childhood to maturity and self-actualization. In psychological terms, modeling heroic ancestral behavior initiates the journey towards self-discovery and individualization. The effective completion of this journey carries the potential for making each one of us a revered ancestor in the collective memory of our descendants. This potential is rooted in the bond of affection between grandparents and grandchildren. In Yoruba culture this bond is called *ifẹ,* which is commonly translated to mean love. I suspect the word has a broader connotation related to the word *Ifá.* If *Ifá* means the wisdom inherent in Nature, the word *ifẹ* suggests the expression of that wisdom in everyday life. As elders we have a responsibility to teach our children and our grandchildren they are essentially good or *ifẹ*, so this message continues to inform future generations.

Ifá says we come to earth to make it a better place for those who follow us (*ire aye*). Based on the Yoruba belief in *atunwa* (reincarnation), future generations include our own return to the Earth we have previously helped shape. This cyclical process is the foundation for both *Ifá* ethics and the *Ifá* view of history. The cycles of birth and rebirth on a personal level are reflected in the movement between creative expansion and destructive contraction that characterizes the traditional African cyclical view of history.

Prior to the emergence of colonialism in Africa, historical accounts of past events were expressed in mythic terms. Myth views history as a cycle of re-occurring events based on universal principles that forever appear, disappear and re-appear. Myth teaches transcendent spiritual principles that can be applied to the unique challenges of each succeeding generation. Earth-centered myth is based on the belief that all of humanity is inter-connected and inter-related. It expresses the metaphysical idea that living in harmony with Nature results in benefit for the individual, the community, the global village and the environment.

Post-colonial myth is rooted in the idea of linear progression and is deeply influenced by the Darwinian concept of "survival of the fittest". In this world-view history is a sequential progression of events leading to greater degrees of progress. The idea of progress is defined as the increased ability to use technology to control Nature. Those who create the most effective technology for exploiting natural resources are considered the fittest from the Darwinian perspective. According to this world-view the fittest are entitled to privilege that ensures the continued linear progression of history. Myth based on this perspective supports the notion that some people are better than others. Consequently there is little attention given to the idea of personal growth and development. Written from a linear perspective, history places emphasis on self-serving justification for acts of greed, exploitation, and conquest. In Western academia the Darwinian approach to history is described as objective because it tends to exclude references to God. The re-occurring message of the Divine Right of the privileged few becomes an unspoken assumption in academia and remains fixed in the consciousness of Western culture as long as it remains effectively unchallenged.

In 1912 the major European colonial powers met in Berlin to create virtually all the boundaries now recognized as sovereign states on the continent of Africa. The purpose for creating these boundaries was to establish spheres of influence for the exploitation of natural resources. Frequently the newly created borders cut across long established, culturally identified, geographical boundaries. In order to sanction the largest expropriation of land since the rise of the Roman Empire, European historians needed to justify this political conquest. The Western academic version of this period of history is based on the premise that European industrial nations brought "progress" and "civilization" to a "backward", "underdeveloped" region that was otherwise devoid of the intelligence needed to develop technological resources. Because this world view has no basis in fact it was necessary to stifle and destroy opposing points of view. The indigenous history of Africa is both written and oral.

The written history was brutalized by deliberately distorting translations of Egyptian hieroglyphics; the oral history was deliberately destroyed by systematic genocide against those elders who were the keepers of traditional ancestral wisdom. From the perspective of *Ifá* in the Diaspora the distortion of history makes it difficult to effectively stand on the shoulders of those who have come before us.

The process of reclaiming the cyclical view of history can begin with a careful examination of the mythic story from *Ifa* oral scripture that gives birth to the tradition of ancestor reverence. In the holy *Odù O̲sa Meji* collected by Pierre Verger in Oyo state Nigeria, the early development of sacred technology associated with ancestor communication reflects a shift in the balance of power between men and women in the culture. The verse gives guidance on how to maintain a healthy balance between genders as part of the stability of the extended family. *O̲sa Meji* also includes symbolic reference to the essential elements used in traditional Yoruba ancestor reverence. The text of the verse is presented in this book as a basis for study, examination and contemplation. My interpretation is just one of many possible contributions to what I hope becomes an on going dialogue. I believe that *Osa Meji* is an important key for an understanding of the *Ifá* concept of family spirit.

Good Character and Reincarnation

The Ifá Concepts of Iwa-pele and Atunwa

IFÁ TEACHES THE IDEA that you cannot know who you are if you cannot call the name of your ancestors going back seven generations. The ability to call the names of your ancestors is believed to make it possible to seat your *ori* (consciousness) in the world. This is a strongly held African worldview related to both the Yoruba concept of good character (*iwa-pe̲le̲*) and the Yoruba concept of reincarnation (*atunwa*).

In an earlier book I translated *iwa-pe̲le̲* to mean good character. The word has that connotation. Yoruba sacred words are often shortened versions of longer phrases. The phrase *iwa ope̲ ile̲* that forms the elision *iwa-pe̲le̲* means, I come to greet the Earth. In traditional Yoruba culture you always greet an elder and an elder is considered a teacher. Having good character means being able to learn form the Earth, and, by extension, being able to live in harmony with the Earth.

The need to live in harmony with the Earth is rooted in the traditional Yoruba concept of *atunwa* meaning character is born again. *Ifá* cosmology includes a belief in reincarnation. According to *Ifá* oral tradition humans reincarnate within their own family lineage, meaning we are the ancestors of our own future incarnations. These fundamental concepts have tremendous impact on Yoruba home training and ethics. We come to greet the Earth and live in harmony with the natural environment so we can make the Earth a better place to live so we will have a comfortable home when we return from the land of the ancestors in a future reincarnation. To be remembered for seven generations is a way to acknowledge personal growth during a particular lifetime, and a way to remember the past accomplishments of a newborn baby. Humans tend to forget previous lives. If the family and the culture preserve that information it becomes an effective tool for guiding future generations who are building on the lessons learned in earlier incarnations. From an *Ifá* perspective spiritual growth involves individual development, family elevation, communal cohesion and global empathy.

Atunwa and *iwa-pe̱le̱* form the theological foundation of *Ifá* ancestor reverence. It is the ancestors who give us guidance in our quest to live in harmony with the Earth, and it is the ancestors who give us guidance in the process of developing good character. These ideas are so fundamental to Yoruba culture that whenever someone is asked a question, no personal opinion is given until there has been a quote from the wisdom of the ancestors in the form of either a proverb or a verse of *Ifá* oral scripture. Personal opinions have little or no value in *Ifa* except as commentary on transcendent ideas.

Calling the name of your ancestors going back seven generations means you will be able to identify your own previous reincarnation. Most children in a traditional Yoruba family have a naming ceremony (*esentaye*) within a week after their birth. The ritual includes divination used to identify the former existence of the child and to establish a connection to either the mother or the father's lineage. This identification gives the developing child solid information on previous lessons. In this way spiritual growth becomes an ongoing process that does not have to start at the beginning with each incarnation. This continuity benefits the individual and the entire community. If we are able to build on the lessons learned in a previous life, we can move on to new lessons that will benefit both self and world. Within the eternal cycle of life, death, transformation and rebirth there is potential for expansion of consciousness symbolized in *Ifá* by the snail shell, a spiral of circular forms gradually increasing in diameter.

To support the on going quest for spiritual elevation *Ifá* honors the spirit of *Egun.* Most books on Yoruba culture translate *Egun* to mean ancestor, which is only partially correct. *Egun* is more accurately defined as the collective consciousness of all those ancestors who are waiting for the opportunity to return to Earth. *Egun,* as a spiritual phenomenon, is bigger and more inclusive than any specific ancestor spirit. The Yoruba word for an individual ancestor would be *Ara O̱run,* meaning body or person living in the Ancestral Realm.

To maintain connection with the collective Spirit of the Ancestors, most traditional Yoruba extended families designate at least one person every generation to be the medium for the family *Egun.* The mediums are called either *Egungun* or *Is̱eg̱un. Egungun* from the elision *e ogun oogun* meaning, I am the medicine of the bones. *Isegun* from the elision *I ase ogun* meaning, I am the power of the bones or, I work the power of the bones. In both instances bones are a symbolic reference to those spirits who have separated from their physical body and returned to the Land of the Ancestors (*Ile Orun*).

In traditional Yoruba culture honoring the ancestors is both a daily discipline and part of the annual ritual calendar. Feeling connected to the ancestors is the glue that holds together the transcendent structure of the extended family while new faces pass through these structures with each new generation. The extended family is transcendent because it functions as a training school for both the development of consciousness and instruction in the specific attributes of good character. The school is set up so that the ten year olds teach the eight year olds; the twelve year olds teach the ten year olds, and so on through parenting and the process of becoming grandparents. As you progress through the natural cycles of growth and maturity your position within the family changes, your responsibilities increase, as does the expectation of mature manifestations of good character.

When *Ifá* was initially brought to the Diaspora through the horrendous denigration of the slave trade, the transcendent structure of the African extended family was deliberately destroyed. This destruction was designed to sustain negative conditioning associating human bondage with the "Will of God". The destructive effect of this shameful dogmatic association continues to plague social dynamics in the West; the decimation of traditional ancestor worship makes the establishment of the extended family as an essential *Ifá* training school an ongoing challenge. It is clear to me that the establishment of Yoruba *Egun* ritual in the Diaspora has been a fundamental step in reclaiming the traditional structure of the *Ifá* extended family across cultural lines.

If we take a verse of *Osa Meji* and examine it closely we find a rich source of information that can be used to inform the practice of *Ifá* as it finds expression in the Diaspora. *Ifá* oral scripture is used as the basic text for divination. In Yoruba culture divination is used as a problem-solving tool as well as a system for preserving the wisdom of the ancestors. The organization of the oracle is based on sixteen fundamental principles called a leg of *Ifá.*

The principle of *Osa* that is the basis for the verses found in *Osa Meji* is the principle of radical change caused by disruptive Forces in Nature. It is the metaphysical idea that Nature is constantly in a state of flux, and that transformation occurs through what is known symbolically and literally as the Winds of Change. Hunters in the Nigerian rain forest say that Spirit moves through the trees on a gust of wind. Whenever a sudden breeze comes through the forest, all the animals in every direction stop and become completely silent. Everything in the forest is adjusting to the shift in spiritual energy moving across the surface of the earth.

In the pre-colonial kingdom of Dahomey, *Osa* was known as the Spirit of Run-away because it is believed to be the metaphysical source of human restlessness. *Osa* is similar to the Tower card in the Tarot Deck because it includes an element of random chaos within the self-regulated flow of any natural environment. Chaos caused by earthquakes, floods, and volcanic eruptions insures a certain level of humility in the relationship between humans and systems that regulate life on Earth. Cataclysmic change may seem harsh and arbitrary to human consciousness, but as an expression of moral change drastic shifts in ecology are often the misunderstood rumblings of a planet looking for stasis and balance. Certain kinds of environmental turbulence are reactions to ecological abuse. The Earth goes through periods of upheaval as a way of wiping the slate clean, in order to eliminate toxins in the process of maintaining fertility, and to preserve the productive balance between earth, air, fire and water.

II II
I I
I I
I I

O̱SA MEJI

(*Iyáàmi* and the Creation of the *Egun* Cloth)

> *O̱sa Meji is rich, a powerful cosmic scream. Ringing bells arrive from the vaults of The Ancestral Realm. Ifá was consulted for Odù on the day Odù was making the journey from Heaven to Earth in the company of Ogun and Obariṣa. Odù was the only women among them. She asked Olodumare what will happen when we arrive in the world? Olodumare said the world would be good. Olodumare said everything they will want to accomplish would be done because he will give them the power. It will be good.*

To say *O̱sa* is a cosmic scream is to identify the principle of *O̱sa* as a fundamental Force in Nature. According to *Ifá* the fundamental Forces in Nature reoccur at different levels of Evolution. The primal winds at the moment of Creation evolve into the solar winds that send elements into the universe, forming planets with ecological systems affected by earthly winds, giving birth to people with an affinity with the Spirit of the Wind. In *Ifá* metaphysics those who have an affinity to the wind are sometimes referred to as *Aje̱*. The word *Aje̱* is sometimes translated to mean, witch and in some literature on *Ifá* it has a negative connotation. *Aje̱* is a person born with the power of the word, the ability to affect Nature through the expression of prayer, and incantations. The power of *Aje̱* is believed to be hereditary passing from mother to daughter. *O̱sa Meji* says women are born with this power; the verse identifies the power as a potent force for good.

From the perspective of Western science the Universe is a giant sine wave and reality comes into being as the result of the effect of sound on light. In other words sound gives light structure. In the words of *Ifá* light is shaped into the visible Universe as a result of the Cosmic Scream. In simple terms sound gives light form.

Lesson 1

Making an Ancestor Pot Washing

IN TRADITIONAL *IFÁ* CULTURE everyone is believed to have the ability, and the obligation to communicate with the ancestors on a daily basis. According to *Ifá* oral tradition, communication with your ancestors is a birthright and requires no special sanction. At times this communication can simply involve remembering a revered ancestor, and using the memory as a basis for making an important decision. In many ways ancestor communication could be defined as an extension of the training and wisdom we receive from our parents and grandparents. In Yoruba culture it is common for the uninitiated to make direct contact with ancestor spirits, the most prevalent method being through dreams. Information also comes by participation in annual ancestor festivals.

In *Ifá* pots with stones are used as a focal point for prayer. No one believes Spirits live in the pot; the belief is that rocks have the ability to amplify prayers. Pots are prepared for various Forces in Nature in a complex system that always follows the same format. Every pot is washed, anointed, invoked, fed and read. The information on how to do this that is associated with *Orisa* is considered taboo to the uninitiated. Most of the information associated with ancestor reverence is in the public domain and can be used as a clear example of the five step process.

In the Diaspora the herbs used to clean sacred objects are frequently referred to as *omiyero*. The word *omiyero* is a reference to snail blood which is a common element used in the washing process. In traditional Yoruba cultural the herbal mixtures used to wash sacred objects are more commonly referred to as either *ewe* meaning herbs, or *Osanyin* meaning Spirit of the Herbs. To wash the elements needed to make an ancestor pot get a large bowl, and a bundle of spinach leaves. Remove the stems from the leaves and place them in the bowl. Say the following prayer over the leaves.

Iba se Egun.

I pay homage to the Spirit of the Ancestors.

Emi (Your Name) *Omo* (list your lineage starting with your parents and working backwards)

I am (your name) child of (lineage)

Iba se Ori Ewe.

I pay homage to the Spirit of the Leaves.

Ko si'ku.

Send away the Spirit of Death.

Ko si arun.

Send away illness

Ko si wahala

Send away all gossip.

Ase

May it be so.

The prayer is spoken directly over the leaves. When the prayer is completed breathe on the leaves and say the word *to* pronounced toe. The word *to* means enough, and is used to indicate the invocation or prayer is completed. This is known as placing your *ase* or spiritual power on the prayer. The word *to* functions as a seal locking the prayer on to the object that is being consecrated or blessed. *To* also indicates the invocation is over so that words spoken after the end of the prayer are not heard by Spirit as part of the prayer.

Add water to the bowl of spinach and tear the leaves into small pieces. Then squeeze the leaves until the water turns green. While squeezing the leaves say the following prayer.

Iba se omi tutu.

I pay homage to the Spirit of Water.

Emi (your name) *Omo* (list your lineage starting with your parents and working backwards).

I am (your name) child of (lineage)

Fun mi,

Bring me,

ire alafia,

the good fortune of peace,

ire l'era,

the good fortune of a stable home,

ire omo,

good fortune to my children

ire owo,

the good fortune of abundance

ire agbo ato,

the good fortune of long life

ire iwa-pele

the good fortune of good character

ire igbodu Egun

the good fortune of an ancestor shrine

ire l'ona iponri atiwo Orun.

the good fortune of the blessing brought by my higher self from the Realm of the Ancestors.

Ase

May it be so.

The prayer should be spoken directly into the water followed by the word *to.*

To make an ancestor pot you need a clay pot at least a foot tall with either a lid or a plate to cover the top, one tiger eye shell which is a large cowry shell with brown dots, five small white cowry shells and the heel from one of your old shoes. Take these ingredients and wash them in the water while singing the following song.

Oyigioyigi ota mi o, Oyigioyigi ota mi o.

The eternal stone of Creation is my foundation.

The eternal stone of Creation is my foundation.

Most songs in traditional Yoruba culture vary from region to region. If you do not know the melody, sing a heart song meaning find a melody that works and sing with feeling.

The Power of the Word

The Ifá Concept of Iyaami

IN TRADITIONAL YORUBA CULTURE the extended family functions as a training school for the family trade, supported by specific sacred traditions. For example, woodcarvers worship *S̱ango* the Spirit of Lightning, blacksmiths worship *Ogun* the Spirit of Iron, cloth makers worship *O̱sun* the Spirit of the River, herbalists worship *Osanyin* the Spirit of Plants and diviners worship *Orunmila* the Spirit of Destiny.

If it is determined during a naming ceremony that a child needs to learn a trade other than the family trade, he or she goes to live with the family that teaches the trade associated with their destiny. This is similar to the concept of a vocational school.

When a person becomes a grandparent they have literally graduated from the family school and become members of the council of elders called *Ogboni.* The word

Ogboni means Wisdom speaks. The elders of *Ogboni* have what would be known in the West as judicial responsibilities. Collectively they settle disputes, enforce traditional laws, monitor religious training and give advice to the King of the village. There are essentially three positions on an *Ogboni* council. The men and women of *Egbe Obatala* have the communal responsibility of developing and maintaining good character (*iwa-pele*). In the verse *Osa Meji* describing the Creation of *Egun* cloth *Egbe, Obatala* is described by the praise name *Obaorisa* meaning King of the Immortals. Enforcement of communal taboo is the responsibility of *Egbe Ogun* who function as blacksmiths, hunters and guardians of the village. A sub group within *Egbe Ogun* called *Oro* has a responsibility to make sure human spirits do not become Earth bound at funerals and they have responsibilities associated with the implementation of capital punishment. The council of female elders is called *Iyaami* literally meaning my mothers. In the verse *Osa Meji* describing the Creation of *Egun* cloth the council of elder mothers is referred to as *Odù*. In the continuation of the verse, *Olodumare* is the Source of everything that becomes manifest in the physical world.

> *Ogun walked in front. When Ogun walked in front Obarisa followed and behind Obarisa came Odù. She asked Olodumare about the world. She said Ogun has the power to fight. He has the gun he has the weapons necessary for victory. She said Obarisa has power, the power of Obarisa makes anything he wants manifest. She said she is the only woman among them and wanted to know her power.*

The Spirit of *Ogun* is associated with the process of transforming the forest into cities, and the process of linking cities through the creation of roads. To say *Obarisa* has the power to make things manifest is to say the King of the Immortals brings us the vision of how people should function within the cities and homes created by *Ogun.* Building a village, a town and a city is more than the random construction of houses. An infrastructure supports the social organization that in turn determines the nature of productivity within a given community. The vision of social organization comes under the sphere of influence of the Spirit known in *Ifá* as *Obarisa.*

In simple terms: the polarity between *Ogun* and *Obarisa* is the polarity between the practical and the political; until recently men dominated both spheres in traditional Yoruba culture. On a metaphysical level *Ogun* and *Obarisa* are both manifestations of the Spirit of Fire. *Ogun* is the fire of the blacksmiths forge, and *Obarisa* is the fire of illumination associated with the sun. Fire is traditionally identified as a masculine Spirit, expansive and transforming. Female Spirits are associated with water, the process of contraction and the ability to nurture. At this point in the verse, *Ifá* scripture asks: what is the relationship between fire and water and how is that relationship reflected in social organization? In the relationship between *Ogun* and *Obarisa* the addition of fire to fire simply produces more fire. The relationship between fire and water creates a new element called steam, making the interaction fundamentally creative.

> *Olodumare said for all of time you will be called Mother. He said you were the only one who traveled to Earth and returned to Heaven. Only the women among them returned. He said you will uphold the world;*

> *Olodumare will give you that power. He said I will give you the power in the form of a bird. Olodumare said it is good.*

According to *Ifá* cosmology women have the ability to communicate directly with Spirit because they know how to use the bird to transcend boundaries of time and space. The bird is a symbol of elemental spirits used by women to trigger astral projection, sometimes referred to as out-of-body experience. Astral projection allows human consciousness to visit the Realm of the Immortals and return to Earthly consciousness. This bifurcated perspective gives *ori* a glimpse of the dual nature of reality.

> *Olodumare asked Odù if she knew how to use the bird in the calabash. Olodumare said you will know how to use it. Odù received the bird from Olodumare and received the power to use it.*

Odù is the Yoruba word for womb, and it is also the word used to describe sacred space. Women understand the dynamics of inter-dimensional travel on a biological level because the womb is a portal between the Earth (*ile aye*) and the Realm of the Ancestors (*ile O̲run*). According to *Ifá* cosmology at the moment of conception the fetus is infused with the Spirit of a lineage ancestor. This Spirit comes through the physical portal of *Odù*. When Spirit becomes manifest at a sacred shrine, the shrine is called *Igbodu* from elision *igbo odu* meaning womb of the forest. The foundation of women's mysteries in *Ifá* is the ability to open the portal of the womb without being pregnant.

Odù departed as she was leaving Olodumare asked her to return. He said come back. He said you Odù when you arrive on Earth how are you going to use the power of the bird, the power I have given you?

Odù said she would fight with the people who would not listen. She said those who do not listen to the will of Olodumare she will fight with them. She said those who would ask for wealth she would give it to them. She said those who wanted children she would give them children. She said if someone receives wealth and become impertinent she will take it away. She said if someone gives birth to a child and they become impertinent she will take it away. She said anything she did for a person if they became impertinent she would take it away.

In traditional Yoruba culture there is a rather strict division of labor based on gender. Men are farmers, women process food, men protect the village from physical threats, and women protect the village from spiritual threats. In the traditional Yoruba extended family the responsibility for maintaining the internal stability of the family is in the hands of the eldest wife.

Olodumare said this is good but you must use this power with calm and for the good.

If you use it for bad things and cause violence, I will reclaim this power. All the men who follow you, I have made you their mother, anything they wish to do they must speak to you first.

To the casual observer traditional Yoruba culture appears to be patriarchal. In Ode Remo, where I was initiated into *Ifá* the women of *Ogboni* must give their blessing to any initiation of a man into *Ifá*. The women also perform key roles in *Ifá* initiation, and without their participation the ritual cannot be completed.

> *It is from this very ancient time that Olodumare has given the power to woman because it was she who received the power of Odù. He gave women the power of the word.*
>
> *Man alone is unable to do anything. Odù arrived in the world. When they all gathered in the world they saw the forest of the dead and it was woman who entered the forest. It was the forest of Oro that woman entered. During this time there was no prohibition against woman entering the forest of Oro. At this time women worshiped all the Orişa. They had full knowledge of all the inner mysteries.*

In Yoruba funeral practice *Oro* is a Spirit of the forest invoked through the use of a bullroarer. At traditional Yoruba funerals the men of *Oro* spin their bullroarers to announce to the spirit of the recently deceased they have made a transition and need to begin the journey to the Ancestor Realm. In ancient times the *Oro* society was the provenance of women but at some point in the history of *Ifa* spiritual practice the mystery of *Oro* was given to men. The men of *Oro* became members of the communal council of elders called *Ogboni*.

> *Woman acted in disgrace and Odù consulted Ifá. The elders said Odù you must act in calm you must have patience, you must not be imprudent. Odù said why? They said because of the power that Olodumare has given you; the people will not know the reason it has been given to you. Odù said she does not know the reason it was given to her. She said she alone was called before Olodumare. She received the power from Olodumare after the others arrived on earth. They said Odù must make offerings to Spirit. She said she would not make offerings to Spirit because the offerings were already made. The offering for woman to receive power was made in the presence of Olodumare. They said she must not become overconfident in joy because she is capable of using these powers for a very long time. The world will not be able to destroy that which she has in her hands. The world will not know the root of her power. Odù refused to make the offering.*

When *Ifá* oral scripture says someone refuses to make an offering, it is explicitly implied that the person is stuck in the arrogant belief they do not need support from the Spirit Realm. According to *Ifá* cosmology arrogance can lead to the loss of spiritual power (*ase*). The flipping back and forth between gender roles represents the social transformation that occurs as a result of the shift between arrogance and humility.

Lesson 2

Making an Ancestor Pot ◆ Anointing ◆

TO ANOINT A POT is to rub material on the pot or stone that will hold the prayers. *Ifá* teaches that words have invisible form in the Universe and certain substances called *ase* can be used to hold words in place in sacred space. The most common forms of *ase* are white chalk, palm oil, honey, molasses, cam wood powder, and charcoal.

For making an ancestor pot the anointing process involves white chalk which is sold in botanicas as either *efun* or *cascaria*. *Efun* is used in traditional Yoruba culture and is petrified sea shells sold in small plugs the size of a thumb. *Cascaria* is a common substitution for *efun* in the Diaspora and is made from bleached egg shells and is sold in small paper cups.

Crush the *efun* or *cascaria* until it looks like talcum powder. Add small amounts of water until the powder forms a sticky clay like substance that can be used as paint. Use the paint to draw and circle and an equal armed cross inside the bottom of the clay pot. Draw the same circle and equal armed cross on the bottom of the lid or plate, meaning the portion of the lid or plate that covers the pot and cannot be seen from outside the pot.

Place an inch of dirt on the bottom of the pot. Then place the heel of your old shoe on top of the dirt. The heel is used to call you back from altered states of consciousness. Cover the heel with an inch of dirt and place the tiger eye shell on the dirt with the open side facing up. Cover the shell completely with dirt. Bring the level of dirt up near the top of the pot and flatten the dirt. Place a single small white cowry shell in the four directions on the dirt and place a single small white cowry shell in the center of the four other shells.

If possible place a small amount of dirt from the grave of an ancestor in each of the quadrants formed by the cowry shells.

Ancestor Masquerade

The Ifá Concept of Egungun

THE WORD *EGUNGUN* REFERS to the family members who hold the sacred responsibility of functioning as mediums for the lineage Ancestral Guardian Spirit (*Egun*). In traditional Yoruba ancestor reverence the mediums wear protective clothing called *Aso Egun;* this protective cloth covers the mediums body completely and keeps them safe while in an altered state of consciousness. Inside the cloth there is an assortment of charms (*iwure*) to both enhance the ability of the medium to access ancestral Spirits, as well as to protect the medium from unwanted spiritual influences. In traditional Yoruba culture it is taboo to identify the person who functions as the medium, even when the identity is common knowledge within the community.

Odù departed without making ebo. She brought the cloth of Egun outside. She brought Oro outside. Obarisa came and said it is the one to whom Olodumare confided, the energetic woman has come to take the world, to take the inner sanctum of Egun and the inner sanctum of Oro and the shrines of all the Orisa. Obarisa would not dare to enter any of these places.

Obarisa consulted Ifá. It was Orunmila who cast Ifa for Obarisa. Orunmila said the message from Olodumare is this: you will take the world in your hands. The world will not be spoiled. No one person will take the world in their hands.

Orunmila is the Spirit of Destiny sacred to those members of the community who train as diviners. This section of the verse speaks of a gender conflict in the history of Yoruba culture over the question of who would be the keepers of certain mysteries, men or women. This issue has shifted throughout history and continues to shift into modern times.

How then will Obarisa be victorious? He consulted Ifa and was told to make an offering to Spirit. Ifá said he must be patient. He must sacrifice snails, a whip-like stick, and cowries. Obarisa made the offering. When Obarisa made the offering Orunmila consulted Ifá. Orunmila said that the world would belong to Obarisa, but you must have patience. He said worship will become yours. He said that which carries the power of woman will be exaggerated. When it is over done she will become your servant. Obarisa understood and said he would have patience.

Ifá is based on the notion of a balance of power between male and female principles. At times this balance is disrupted by an over emphasis on one side or the other as social situations cause tension and an ebb and flow in the balance of power.

All of the customs, those that are good and those that are bad, brought to earth by Odù with the power given to her by Olodumare include the taboo against looking at her material form. If the taboo is violated she will make the person blind. If she says the gaze of someone is evil, if she says a person is going to have a headache, they will have a headache, if she says they will have stomach pain, they will have stomach pain. All things said by Odù will come to pass.

In traditional Yoruba culture it is taboo for anyone to see the sacred ritual objects that are used by a specific religious society unless the person is initiated into that society. Here the verse is indicating the consequences of violating the taboo.

When the time came Odù said Obarisa we have come to earth together. She said come they had come to the same place. She said if we are in the same place she would allow Obarisa to see anything she wanted to do.

This is a reference to a historical time when men learned *awo* (sacred technology) from women.

> *Odù said because Obariṣa and Ogun fell from the sky together they chose Ogun to be a warrior. Those who wanted to make war would not be victorious against Ogun.*
>
> *Odù and Obariṣa needed to live together in one place. At the place where they came together they must stay. The snail offered by Obariṣa was used to praise his head at the place where he lived. The liquid from the snail was used to drink. Obariṣa did not want to drink the water from the snail. Odù drank the water from the snail and her stomach became calm. She told Obariṣa that because of him she had discovered something delicious to eat. She said the snail water is sweet and the snail itself is sweet. When she finished eating she said it was good. She said no one has ever given me anything as good to eat as a snail. She said a snail is what one must give me to eat.*

Snail blood called *omiyero* is used by those who worship *Obariṣa* to clean their heads and is used by worshippers of *Odu* as ingested medicine.

> *Odù said the same snail that is given to you must be given to me.*

In *Ifá* cosmology the snail has a cooling effect and coolness is believed to be the key to cooperation, especially cooperation between the genders.

> *Obarisa said he would give Odù snails. He said the power you do not give me bothers me. He asked her to show him the things she possessed. She said when he comes to live with her in one place he must not hide anything from her. She said she would not hide anything from him. She said he will see all of her works and procedures. She said we will live in one place. Obarisa said this was not bad.*
>
> *Odù brought the things needed to worship Egun into the inner sanctum of Egun. She said Obarisa should follow. He said he was afraid. She said follow her and he followed her. When Obarisa followed her he entered the forest of Egun. They worshipped Egun together. But she did not show him how to make the sound of Egun.*

This is a reference to a time when men wanted to learn the mysteries women brought from the Realm of the Ancestors to Earth as a result of their ability to astral travel. The refusal by women to show men how to make the sound of *Egun* is a refusal to show men the secret of how to become a medium.

> *Odù did not know how to make the voice of Egun. She did know how to speak with the Immortals in Heaven. When they worshipped*

Egun Odù took the cloth. She covered herself and gave thanks for her nourishment. When she finished her propitiations she left. The time had come for her and Obarisa to go to their dwelling place. Obarisa went to the place of the cloth. The cloth of Egun did not have cloth streamers. He added the streamers. The streamers allowed Egun to see. When women made Egun the cloth was simple and the made the face in a way that did not allow Egun to see. When Obarisa arrived he added the streamers. Before they reached their home Obarisa went to the rear court of Egun. He took the cloth of Egun and cut the face opening and placed streamers in the opening. When this was done he covered himself with the cloth. He took a whip into his hands but he did not say goodbye to Odù. He said he was going to the rear court of Egun, the place where Egun came out. Obarisa spoke with the voice of Egun and they did not recognize his voice. He said his prayers and Egun said Hen. He said Ha. One who wished to praise Egun says Hen and he said Ha. He said the Egun he praises is infallible. He said when he came from Heaven to Earth one of the people from Heaven came to earth with him. He took the whip and dragged it on the ground. At his home he spoke with the voice of Egun and Odù became frightened. When she brought the cloth she did not know this way of speaking. She asked who has entered this cloth, who speaks too quickly and with such a voice? With insight men take power.

Egun mediums were originally women and at some point men took over the *Egun* dance. The male mediums that are initiated into the mystery of *Egungun* speak in a high-pitched falsetto voice when they are in possession with the Spirit of *Egun.*

Recently the elders in Ile Ife have opened the initiation for *Egun* to women. This is not an innovation as much as it is a return to an earlier practice, part of the eternal cycle of life, death, transformation and rebirth.

Lesson 3

Making an Ancestor Pot Invocation

ORIKI IS THE YORUBA WORD for invocation, literally translated it means praise the head, or praise the consciousness of a particular Spirit. In the context of *Ifá* ritual you need to invite specific Spirits to participate in any ceremonial process. Ritual in *Ifá* tends to follow a set sequence; invite Spirit to the sacred space, make an offering to Spirit to acknowledge the acceptance of the invitation, ask Spirit for guidance, close the ritual and return to the mundane world.

Some of the *Ifá* rituals for Forces in Nature (*Oriṣa*) are very formal and stylized requiring a strict adherence to structure, form and content. These rituals have been passed down through generations; due to a familiar resonance with the invitation, it is the preservation of a set formula that helps draw the Spirit being invoked. The situation is different with the invocation of ancestors. Not everyone involved in *Ifá* worship has ancestors who are familiar with traditional Yoruba invocations. This means there is no correct way to call the ancestors of your lineage. There are only effective and ineffective methods of communication. We can use the traditional Yoruba style of invocation as a guideline to discover what works for our personal ancestors. The invocations in this lesson are for use with a personal ancestor shrine, for making an ancestor pot and may be used for public rituals involving *Egungun* Masquerade.

Invocations for the ancestors are traditionally followed by a recitation of the ancestral lineage of the person who is saying the invocation. The name of the ancestor is preceded by the phrase *Iba se* followed by the name of the ancestor. In traditional *Ifá* ancestor invocations the name of the ancestor is followed by a short poetic phrase describing the significant accomplishments of the person named. For anyone who is new to the tradition and who has no family *oriki,* the task of writing short poetic descriptions of their ancestors can be challenging and rewarding. It is challenging because it might involve extensive research; it is rewarding because it becomes a part of family oral history and be passed on to future generations.

It is appropriate to recite the family history portion of the invocation in the language most familiar to the ancestors. Because many of us have limited information on family history it has become traditional in the Diaspora to recite the ways in which you imagine your ancestors may have crossed over as a way of remembering unknown ancestors.

Some *Ifá/Orisa* communities in the Diaspora have developed their own traditions associated with ancestor reverence, and these should be honored and maintained by members of those extended families who have preserved a particular legacy.

While reciting invocations to the ancestors it is traditional to pour libation; it may be either water or some type of alcohol. In Africa it is common to pour alcohol into the cap of the bottle then use a finger to dribble small amounts on the floor. In the Diaspora it is common to take a drink then spray the alcohol on the shrine.

Use this *oriki* to call the ancestors once your pot has been washed and anointed. It can also be used to invite your ancestors to speak once the pot is in place.

ORÍKÌ EGÚN

(Praising the Ancestors, invocation for consecration of Ancestor shrine)

Egúngún kiki egúngún.

Praise to the mediums of the Ancestors.

Egún ikú ranran fe̱ awo ku opipi.

Ancestors who have preserved the mystery of featherless flight.

O da so bo fun le̱ wo.

You create the words of reverence and power.

Egún ikú bata bango egún de̱.

The drums of the Ancestors announce the arrival of the Ancestors.

Bi aba f'atori na le̱ egún as̱e̱ de̱. As̱e̱.

On the strong mat you spread your power the Ancestors are here. May it be so.

* This is an effective invocation for possession by ancestor spirits. It is also used for the consecration of an ancestor shrine.

Following the initial invocation it is traditional to call the name of our known ancestors. It is also traditional in some areas for men to begin the recitation of ancestors by starting with the lineage of their father working backwards before reciting the lineage of their mother. Women would start with the lineage of their mother and work backwards before starting with the lineage of the father. I prefer listing the names from the most recently departed to the most distant departed. Some lineages work from the most distant known ancestor to the most recently departed. Again there is no correct way only personal preference.

There are two reasons for calling the ancestors: the first is to invite them to be present at the ancestor shrine and the second is to preserve their memory. In Yoruba culture the *oriki* of a particular family is an important oral record of family history and of the accomplishments of specific ancestors. Our task as elders and ancestors of future generations is to preserve that history. The information we gather and incorporate into our ancestor invocation will be remembered and passed on to our children as a way of preserving the memory of lineage accomplishments. In Yoruba culture *Ifá* teaches the idea that no one can know who they are if they cannot call their ancestors going back seven generations. *Ifá* also teaches that anyone who is remembered for seven generations into the future has achieved immortality.

After saying a traditional *oriki* I start by calling my paternal grandfather, Adelburt Fenyes. I say, "*Iba se* Dr. Adelburt Fenyes, the man who studied medicine in Vienna, lived in Cairo and moved to Pasadena where he opened a doctor's office with the city's first X-Ray machine". In this way I call his name, remember some of his accomplishments and preserve the memory for my children. Writing an ancestor *oriki* should involve some thought, some study, some research and some inspiration from the ancestors. As we learn more about our ancestors we can add to the *oriki,* they are not etched in stone. Developing an ability to communicate with ancestors generates new information and a new understanding of their accomplishments. Information generated by the ancestors can and should be incorporated into the invocation process.

Every family has their share of uninspiring ancestors. If you know a particular ancestor suffered from substance abuse, and or extremely destructive behavior, their names do not need to be included in the invocation process. The ancestors we invoke will influence our behavior. We do not need the influence of child molesters, drug dealers and sociopathic criminals.

Following the recitation of known ancestors, it is traditional to list the unknown ancestors by praising the ways in which you imagine image some of them may have crossed over. For example;

Iba se all those who passed in the middle crossing.

Iba se all those who died in childbirth.

Iba se all those who died in war.

Iba se all those who died of illness.

At this point in the invocation process it is traditional to include a song. It may be a traditional Yoruba ancestor song, or it may be a religious song familiar to your ancestors, such as a hymn, spiritual, or you may choose to sing portions of the Koran, or portions of the Torah. While singing you might feel the impulse to dance. The traditional Yoruba ancestor dance step involves turning the right foot to the right, then moving the left heel towards the instep of the right foot. When dancing for the ancestors the legs never cross. The body is generally tilted forward and the arms swing freely. Dance movements in *Ifá* are similar in purpose to postures used in yoga; the dance step is designed to make the person receptive to the *ase* that is being invoked.

Once the invocation process is completed it is common practice to leave an offering. Traditionally the offering would be a portion of the meal prepared for the living family on the day you speak to the ancestors. This can be placed on the altar or on the floor in front of the altar.

At this point in the ritual you are ready to speak to the ancestors. The first words might be to ask for their blessing. In Yoruba you could say, *ire omo, ire owo, ire agbo ato* meaning good fortune to my children, good fortune of abundance, and the good fortune of a long healthy life. I find that talking to the ancestors is more effective if you ask a single question and sit quietly waiting for an answer. It is not necessary to experience strange phenomena, or even go into an altered state of consciousness to communicate with the ancestors even though these things sometimes happen. If you have a problem and you present it to the ancestors and ask for their assistance the solution may come in many forms. The simplest form of communication with the ancestors is remembering how a particular ancestor may have resolved a particular problem. After the problem has been presented to the shrine, the answer may come from the ancestors in unexpected ways in the course of the days that follow. It is up to us to be vigilant so we can recognize the answer in whatever forms it takes. The prayer portion of ancestor rituals comes after the *oriki* and is called *aladura* from the elision *ala dudu ra* meaning bring light to darkness.

The Elemental Spirit of the Birds

The Ifá Concept of Eleiye

WHEN THE BRITISH colonial empire invaded Nigeria and took control of the country to exploit the natural resources they made a very precise study of *Ifá* culture. As a result of their study they determined that the easiest way to disrupt the traditional Yoruba political structure was to outlaw *Ogboni.* When they disbanded the elder's council the British were able to select Yoruba Kings and Queens and to place them in positions of power without fear they would be deposed through the traditional judicial process.

In an effort to maintain economic control after relinquishing political power the British sponsored a Christian Crusade in the early 1950s for the purpose of systematically burying the remnants of the traditional Yoruba women's secret societies. The sacred icon of these societies was the Spirit of a bird. As a result of this denigration, the women became understandably secretive about their relationship to the Spirit of the bird.

> *Olodumare first gave the wisdom to women and he gave the power of the birds to women. When Odù saw that Egun had a whip in hand she ran away. Obaris̱a carried the Egun and entered the town. Odù saw the cloth was her own. She asked is that Obaris̱a? She remained in her house and sent her bird on a mission. She said the wing must rest on the shoulder of Egun. They must go together. Everything that Egun says will be activated by the power of the bird perched on his shoulder. When everything he says has become manifest he will return to the rear court of Egun.*

There is a common notion in the Diaspora that *Egungun* ritual is the sole providence of men. This segment of the verse is saying the power of the male *Egun* society is supported by the power of the women's society. Before the men go out in public to dance with the *Egun* cloth the women who worship the Spirit of the bird place the men in possession by calling the Guardian Spirit of the Ancestors. The women's contribution to the process is done in secret inside the Ancestor Shrine.

> *Obaris̱a undressed on the ground. He placed his whip on the ground. He dressed himself. He left. The bird went to its owner. When Obaris̱a came home he was greeted by Odù. She said welcome. She said where did you come from? Obaris̱a said he came from*

> *outside. Odù said that is good. You are welcome.*

It is taboo to know the identity of *Egun* mediums. This is a subtle reference to the taboo because the woman is pretending she does not know the identity of the medium.

> *Obarisa dumped all of his things on the ground and Odù said this was good. She said it is the Egun cloth that you have taken outside. Obarisa said yes. Odù said it is good. She said you have shown me what I must do. She said people behold Egun. She dragged the whip over the ground and said the honor is for you. She said today I will leave. She said I concede Egun to man. She said because of me no woman will ever dare to enter into the Egun cloth she said she has given the Egun to men. She said he must go outside with Egun because she has the power that Egun utilizes. She said Egun is compatible with the birds. At the place where Egun manifests, there also the birds appear. All the power used by Egun comes from the birds. Odù said no woman will ever enter the Egun cloth, but she will be able to dance, to meet Egun and dance in front of Egun if Egun is outside. She said Egun departs today and it is man who will guide Egun.*

Again to the uninitiated it would appear that *Egun* worship is male dominated. This verse is saying that *Egun* is supported by the power of women both prior to taking

Egungun out into the public and while the *Egungun* is in public.

> *Odù said all things the people wish to do are aided by women. That is why men are unable to do anything on Earth, if they do not obtain the hand of woman.*
>
> *They chanted, on the fifth day they celebrated the week. They said all the incantations they would chant would come from the holy Odù Ifá called Osa Meji.*

The power of women in *Osa Meji* is the gateway to the land of the ancestors. The traditional Yoruba calendar is based on a four-day week, which is called a five-day week because the fifth day and the first day are counted together. The verse is saying that the power of the ancestors is invoked every four days to maintain the connection with *Egun* whether or not the *Egungun* dancer comes out in public.

> *They said they will praise the women, they said if they praise the women the Earth will be tranquil. They chanted:*

> *Prostrate, prostrate for the women.*
>
> *Woman has placed you in the World, thus you are humanity.*
>
> *Woman is the intelligence of the Earth,*
>
> *prostrate for woman.*

Woman has placed you in the World, thus you are humanity.

In *Ile Ife* the sacred city of Yoruba culture the traditional *Egungun* dancers who wear the Ancestral cloth includes the initiation of women. This represents a return to the early traditions when women originated the dance.

Lesson 4

Making an Ancestor Pot ◆ Offering ◆

AFTER THE WASHING, anointing, and invocation of the pot, it is traditional to feed the pot. If you are an *Ifá* or *Oris̱a* initiate the pot may be fed a pigeon in the tradition manner. Everyone else should make a food offering to the pot. The Yoruba term for this type of offering is *adimu egun.* The idea behind making an offering is reciprocity. If we ask the ancestors for their guidance we need to give them something in return. Offering food is not meant to literally feed a Spirit; it is meant as a gesture of honoring the memory of those who once ate with us.

In Africa the most common offering to the ancestors is a small portion of every meal placed on the edge of the eating mat. In Western culture meals are generally eaten at a table, the offering to the ancestors may be placed on a small plate that is set on the floor in front of the *Egun* altar or it may be placed on the altar directly. It is traditional in the Diaspora to use a plate with a crack. The broken plate is symbolic of the body that is discarded when the human soul (*emi*) is elevated.

In addition to food, it is traditional to offer something to drink. A cup of coffee, tea, or alcohol may be placed next to the plate. If you are pouring libation hold the bottle with the left hand and cover the spout with your thumb and sprinkle a few drops on the floor. Flowers can also be used as an offering and they can be placed directly on the altar. It is common practice in the Diaspora to use cigars as offerings to the ancestors. The smoke is used as a method of cleansing similar to smudge. Once you are in communication with the ancestors they will make specific requests for the kinds of offerings they want. You should make every effort to comply with the request, because in my experience it will enhance the quality of communication.

After making the offering thank the ancestors for all the blessings you have already received. You may express your thanks in your own words or you may use the following Yoruba *oriki* (praise poem)

E nle oo rami o.

I am greeting you my friends.

Be ekolo ba juba ile a lanu.

If the earth worm pays homage to the earth the earth always gives it access.

O̱mo̱de ki ijuba ki iba pa a.

A child who pays homage never suffers the consequences.

Egun mo ki e o.

Ancestors I greet you.

Egun mo ki e o ike eye.

Ancestors I greet you with respect.

Ohun ti wo ba njhe lajule Orun.

Whatever good things are being eaten in the realm of the ancestors,

No mo ba won je.

Eat my offering with them.

J'epo a t'ayie sola n'igbale.

Eat richly from the earth.

Omo a t'ayie sola n-igbale.

The children of the earth are grateful for your blessing.

Ori Egun, mo dupe.

I thank the wisdom of the ancestors.

Ase.

May it be so.

Feeding the ancestors should be done on a regular basis to keep them close to your shrine. The frequency of the feeding is part of the agreement you make with your ancestors. In Africa some elders make an offering to *Egun* at every meal and before they drink any liquids. In the Diaspora it is more common to make an offering once a week at the shrine. It can be effective to feed the ancestors less frequently as long as you keep to your schedule and your agreement.

For those who have not been initiated, having an ancestor shrine will provide a place to use the system of four cowries for divination. It will also give access to ancestor spirits who will speak through divination. In all the systems of divination based on *dafa* (*Odù Ifá*), the divination is directed towards a specific Spirit. That Spirit may bring messages from a number of sources, but the invocations to open divination are always directed to either a particular *Egun* or *Orisa*.

Gender Roles in Traditional Yoruba culture

The Ifá Concept of Iyanifá

IFÁ TEACHES THAT EVERY *ODÙ* emerges from its opposite polarity. This means light transforms into darkness, and darkness transforms into light. For example the *odu* *Ose'tura* appears as follows.

```
I   I
II  II
I   I
I   II
```

The single lines symbolize light and the double lines symbolize darkness. This is not a polarity between good and evil, it is a polarity between expansive and contractive

Forces in Nature. If we take *Ose ´tura* and transform every double line into a single line and every single into a double line we get the *Odù Ofun Ika.*

II II

I I

II II

II I

There is a fundamental relationship between these two *Odù*. *Ose'tura* is the ability of humans to project their prayers into the Realm of the Immortals. *Ofun Ika* is the ability of the Immortals to answer our prayers. If we count the number of single marks in both *Odù* we get a total of eight single marks. If we count the number of double marks in both *Odù* we get eight double marks. Single lines represent expansive *ase* or spiritual power symbolized in *Ifá* scripture as Male Spirits. Double lines represent contractive *ase* or spiritual power symbolized in *Ifá* scripture as Female Spirits. In the polarity between *Ose'tura* and *Ofun Ika* we find perfect balance between forces of expansion and forces of contraction.

If you take any *Odù* and mark its opposite then add the number of single and double lines in both *Odù* the total is always eight single lines and eight double lines. *Odù* are two dimensional representations of three dimensional energy patterns. According to *Ifá* all energy patterns evolve out of their opposite polarity. Einstein expressed this idea in his theory of conservation of energy. He stated that energy in the Universe is neither created nor destroyed it is only transformed. The transformation of energy evolves from a condition called stasis meaning a balance between opposites. In Western science the idea of expansive energy is called electromagnetism and the idea of contractive energy is called gravity.

As a principle of science if the energy of electromagnetism was stronger than the energy of gravity the universe would evolve into a beam of light. If the energy of gravity was stronger than the energy of electromagnetism the universe would collapse into a black hole. The Universe exists as a result of the balance of power between structure or gravity and dynamics or electromagnetism. In *Ifa* scripture this polarity is symbolized by the balance of power between Male and Female Spirits and is coded into the marks used to represent the two hundred and fifty six fundamental Forces in Nature called *Odù*.

Ifá ritual is a stylized enactment of metaphysical principles based on the movement of polar tension towards resolution and balance. To the casual observer Yoruba culture can appear to be patriarchal. What is often not seen is the *Ifá* principle that the person in charge changes depending on what you are doing. When we see traditional Yoruba families together in public the eldest male is clearly the chief. I believe this is for purposes of security and to facilitate protection of the family. Inside the house the balance of power shits to the eldest mother. In public *Ifá* initiates are treated as the eldest leaders in the community because divination is considered the clearest form of communication with Spirit and Spirit is believed to guide the development of good character. Behind closed doors, at *Ogboni* rituals used to settle disputes, *Obatala* initiates function as chief because of their innate sense of fairness. This is in stark contrast to the Western model of family organization where the male is the chief in all matters. The Western model of family organization is an extension of the corporate model of the CEO who is in charge of everything both of which are expressions of the patriarchal notion of God the Father. In the Diaspora the overwhelming influence of the idea of God the Father makes an understanding of the *Ifá* idea of God the Father/Mother challenging.

When I first started the study of *Ifá* in the late eighties as a member of the *Orisa* community in the Diaspora my exposure to *Ifá* was limited. There were *Ifá* communities in New York, Miami and Los Angeles. These families were predominately Spanish speaking Cubans who did not teach or initiate outside their culture. In the nineties those who were interested in *Ifá* from an African perspective were blessed by the teachings of Chief Abimbola, Chief Fatunmise and Chief FAMA who took large numbers of Americans to Africa for initiation into *Ifá* and made the tradition available on a cross cultural basis.

It has been my observation that the sudden and widespread interest in reclaiming the lost aspects of *Ifá* in the Diaspora created an understandable and well founded concern among the women of the *Orisa* communities that the tradition was running the risk of becoming excessively patriarchal. In an effort to establish some level of gender balance the interest in *Ifá* among men has stimulated an interest in the female initiations associated with *Ifá* in traditional Yoruba culture.

In my lineage in Ode Remo there are four initiations for women in *Egbe Ifá: Asarepawo, Asawo, Aworo* and *Apetebi*. Because of the extreme persecution of traditional religion in Nigeria in general and because women have been selected by Christian evangelists as easy targets, traditional Yoruba women are very reluctant to discuss the details of these various positions. Based on my experience I would suggest that *Asarepawo* is the beginning level of initiation for women in Ode Remo and essentially means someone who is in training to become *Asawo*. The word *Asawo* is an elision of *ase awo*. The word *ase* has many meanings based on context and can be a reference to food for Spirit. In my experience in Ode Remo the men of *Egbe*

Ifá slaughter most of the meat used in ritual and the women prepare the food in ways that make the food a form of spiritual medicine. During initiations *ase* food is prepared for both the initiates and for Spirit.

Aworo is an elision of *awo oro* meaning the mystery of the power of the word. The women of *Aworo* are sanctioned by *Ifá* to say *oriki* related to *Ifá* ritual to assist with the divination process and assist in making *ebo.*

In the *Ifá* of Ode Remo there is no initiation specifically called *Iyanifá.* The full initiation for *Ifá* called *tefá* is for men only. The purpose of *tefá* is to unlock the female potential inside a man so the man becomes fully developed as a person. There are initations in Ode Remo which unlock the male potential in a woman making them fully developed as a person. This does not mean that *Iyanifá* is wrong, invalid or inappropriate. In my opinion what is commonly called *Iyanifá* in the Diaspora is very similar to what is called *Aworo* in Ode Remo. Titles are subject to regional differences in dialects. What is important is a metaphysical understanding of the role of men and women in *Ifá* as expressed by *Odù* in general and to examine the shift in women's roles as expressed in the *Odù Osa Meji.*

When I bring someone to Ode Remo for *Ifá* initiation the *Araba* consults with the elder mothers to make sure they approve of the candidate. Prior to the initiation the female elders of Ode Remo visit the male novice and admonish him to become a man of good character, a man worthy of their trust and support. During the initiation the women of *Ifá* surround the sacred grove to protect the initiate from spiritual intrustion. As the initiate leaves the sacred grove to return to the village the women of *Ifá* make offerings along the road in front of his course of travel to make sure he arrives home safely. At the end of the initiation *ikin,* the sacred seeds of *Ifá* are presented to various places on the body of a female initiate to insure that the seeds are fully consecrated. To complete the initiation a female *Ifá* initiate takes the cloths of the male novice to absorb the negativity cleaned off him during the initiation. The negative is grounded by the women through their menstrual cycle.

The role of female *Ifá* initiates in Ode Remo is to clearly support the transformation process of the male initiates. In social political terms it is a secondary role. Parity comes when the men of *Ifá* support the initiations designed to balance and elevate the spirit of women. The problem in studying and understanding the full equity of women in *Ifá* culture is that traditional Yoruba women tend to honor the taboo against discussing female mysteries in public, making it difficult to determine what takes place behind the veil of secrecy.

The taboo against speaking in public is reinforced by the vicious denigration of female mysteries propagated by Christian churches in Nigeria. During the mid fifties there was a Christian Crusade that moved through Nigeria with the express purpose of destroying all in the traditional female religious societies in Yoruba culture. Many villages in Yoruba land are built near an *oroko* tree and the trees are used as shrines for many of the traditional women's mysteries. William Bascom documented the Christian Crusade on film as it traveled from village to village burning *oroko* trees; smashing sacred pots and destroying ancient alter objects.

The Crusade preceeded the British abdication of direct colonial control over Nigeria. In retrospect the assault on women's mysteries appears to have had a political rather than a spiritual motive. In traditional Yoruba culture there are twenty-one *Oba* or kings. The crown of the kings is a conical shaped beaded hat decorated with sixteen birds. The conical shape symbolizes the womb or *Odù.* The sixteen birds represent the power of feminine manifestation as it is expressed through the sixteen metaphysical principles used as the basis for *Ifá* divination. The women of the communities ruled by each of the kings have variously named secret societies that have responsibility for the care and feeding of the crown. If the *Oba* violates any taboo of his office the women use the threat of refusing to relinquish the crown as an effective tool for maintaining ethical political behavior. The British Government wanted these women out of power so that they could affect the political process after the "official" end of colonialism in Nigeria.

The problem for those of us who worship *Ifá* in the Diaspora is to find a way to learn the *awo* associated with female spiritual power without jeopardizing the safety and security of our elder mothers in Nigeria and without patronizing the elder mothers in newly developing communities. As an *awo* part of my responsibility to Ode Remo is to pass on the oral aspects of the tradition to future generations. This position has given me access to some, but not all the inner secrets of our elder mothers. The need for some understanding of these mysteries is essential for any *awo* who is actively engaged in the divination process to refer women to the rituals needed for their development and growth.

For me the key to understanding *Ifá* metaphysics is an examination of *awo* Yoruba, the language of *Ifá* scripture. The Yoruba word for female spiritual power is *ge* which I believe is a reference to female fertility. The word *ge* is the foundation for a number of elisions that make reference to women's mysteries. The word *gele* is an elision of *ge ile* meaning house of fertility and is used to describe the head wraps worn by traditional Yoruba women. When members of an extended family are in public for a formal occasion all the women wear the same cloths. The woman with the highest *gele* is the eldest mother in the family and the person who is greeted first when you encounter the family as a group.

The word *g<u>e</u>lefun* is used in some regions of Yoruba land to describe communal women's societies. The word is an elision of *g<u>e</u> ile ofun* meaning the house of fertility brings manifestation from the Immortals.

G<u>e</u>d<u>e</u> from the elision *g<u>e</u> did<u>e</u>* meaning female power arises is the word used in *Ifá* to describe topographical astrology. In *Ifá* topographical astrology is used to identify times when *igbodu,* the sacred groves, are open to spiritual power from the invisible realm. The word *igbodu* is from the elision *igbo odù* meaning womb of the forest. The word *Odù* is used to describe both the sacred pot used in *Ifá* initiations and the portal that allows the spirit of a baby to enter the mother's womb.

There are a number of words that are frequently used interchangeably that do not have the exact same meaning in the context of *Odù Ifá.* The word *Aj<u>e</u>* which is often translated to mean witch is actually the power of the word which is passed from mother to daughter. The original English meaning of the word witch was wise women, but the word has taken on a negative pejorative meaning in post Christian Western culture. The *Aj<u>e</u>* are often accused of causing disruption in the form of the collective anger of women. Too often the assumption is that this is a negative phenomenon. Disruption of that which is no longer effective is part of the natural cycle of progress and change. *Aj<u>e</u>* is not a spirit per se and is not given as a pot in most regions of Yoruba land. It is the inherited aptitude for effective invocation. The single most powerful Force in Nature in the development of any child is the voice of the mother. This power is called *Aj<u>e</u>.*

Eleiye is the Yoruba word for bird. In the context of *Odù Ifá eleiye* is a reference to the sacred technology used to facilitate out of body experience. The elemental spirit of a bird is given to men and woman to teach the process of separating our visual perceptions from our physical body.

During the initiation for *eleiye* the spirit of a bird is ingested and when the person wants to travel in the Invisible Realm the spirit of the bird is used as a guide.

Anyone, man or woman who has the ability to astral travel has what *Ifá* calls *oṣo*. References to *Iyaami Oṣoranga* only make sense in terms of the elision *Iya mi Oṣo ran ga* meaning the mothers who astral travel. This is a description of the collective *aṣe* of women in a community which may or may not be part of an organized secret society.

Odù Ifá refers to those who have learned the mysteries associated with women's power as *Obinrin Irun* meaning bearded women. This is a reference to post menopausal women or to elder grandmothers. Traditional Yoruba culture has a strict division of labor based on gender to facilitate the rigors of life in the rain forest. Men farm, women process the food. Men harvest the farm; women sell the excess food at the market. Fathers physically protect the men and women of the village. Grandmothers spiritually protect the men and women of the village. Grandfathers care for and teach the children as do women of child bearing age. In this way each gender has a time in their life for nuturing children and for protecting the family.

To fully understand these mysteries requires male initiates in the Diaspora to let go of the culturally conditioned need to be in charge. *Ifá* initiation does not put a man in a position of power to control the community. This is an imposition of a Christian idea to an African world view. The foundation of *Ifá* is the ability to surrender to the will of Spirit. In Ode Remo the male initiates of *Ifá* are mediums of the Spirit *Ela*. The *aṣe* or spiritual power of *Ela* is unformed consciousness that emerges from the Invisible Realm through sacred portals called *Igbodu*. The light of *Ela* is projected from the *awo* back to the Invisible Realm through the use of *oriki* which are invocations that give shape and substance to what is originally unformed consciousness. The answer to our prayers comes back to the visible realm through the portal of *Odù*. This portal is symbolized by the *Odù* pot given to elder *awo*. The portal exists in reality in the womb of the mothers and the mystery of the mothers is the ability to open this portal for ritual purposes. There exists in this relationship a sacred polarity between men and women that reflects the sacred polarity that exists throughout Creation. The process of finding the balance needed to make effective use of this polarity is the process of developing trust.

My *ita,* the divination done at the time of my initiation into *Ifá* stated that I had an obligation to bring lost aspects of *Ifá* to my community in the Diaspora including some of the lost women's mysteries. This has been a source of added confusion to an already clouded issue. When a male *awo* gives *Eleiye* he must enter an altered state of consciousness that gives him access to the *as̱e* of *Iyaami O̱soronga.* This is a difficult and challenging, but not impossible, altered state for a man to hold. *Odù Ifá* says that men travel safely in the land of the Mothers by dressing like a bird. This is a symbolic reference to a specific altered state of consciousness. Once I passed the information I received in Africa about women's mysteries to women, my involvement in the process was over. They conduct the initiations and I assume a supportive role based on what the women say they need from me. Just as the women of *Aworo* support the initiation of men into *Ifá,* the men of *Ifá* support the *awo* of *ge̱lefun.*

It is my observation that *Ifá* initiations for women coupled with initiations that are specifically for women are the keys to creating parity between the genders. Others may disagree. There is little doubt that the issue of gender equity is a source of tension and conflict within our communities. *Odù Ogbe Ogunda* gives us clear guidance on how to resolve this tension in an effort to create balance.

Orunmila cast Ifá for the novice on the day the novice provoked the anger of the mothers. The novice said Baba how do I appease the anger of the mothers? Orunmila said it is the Odundun leaf that you use to appease the anger of the mothers. The novice looked everywhere for the Odundun leaf and found it nowhere. After many years of travel the novice returned to the shrine of Orunmila and said Baba I have searched everywhere for the Odundun leaf and I can find it nowhere. Baba tell me what is the Odundun leaf? Baba said the Odundun leaf is whatever the mothers say it is.

Lesson 5

Making an Ancestor Pot Divination

Part 1

WHEN WE SPEAK OF *IFÁ*, the word has two meanings. *Ifá* is the Yoruba word for the Wisdom of Nature. Anything you can learn about yourself or the world from a Yoruba language perspective is *Ifá*. When you talk to a traditional Yoruba elder, and you say something about Western science, psychology, or cars, or anything that involves knowledge of the world that is considered *Ifá,* even if the inventor of the airplane was not an *Ifá* priest the invention would be considered *Ifá*.

The word *Ifá* also refers to a religious tradition that emerged out of a West African city called Ile Ife̱. This tradition is based on observations of natural law. The wisdom taught by Nature is the basis for the religious belief which is the foundation of traditional Yoruba culture. The concept of Yoruba culture is limited because the word *Yoruba* was invented by Jesuits. It was a way to identify a certain group of people who spoke a particular language, from a common root. This language group was identified so the Bible could be translated into what is now known as the Yoruba language. The translators arbitrarily decided the Yoruba of Oyo was the standard and based their translations on this particular dialect. No real effort has ever been made to create a dictionary of liturgical Yoruba, meaning a compilation of terms used in traditional Yoruba sacred scripture.

Within *Ifá* there is a complex system for identifying Forces in Nature. The system is based on the belief that everything in Nature has consciousness. If everything has consciousness, then potentially we can communicate with everything. In a sense, the Forces in Nature are limitless. *Ifá* recognizes that different levels of Creation, from the Big Bang to fish in the ocean, to people on the surface of the earth, make use of similar principles for organizing consciousness. There is the consciousness of fire that is at the center of the earth, the consciousness of fire that creates the sun, the consciousness of fire that created the big bang at the beginning of time, and the consciousness of fire is also described as the passion for social justice. You can be a person who has a physical body with a consciousness that is structured by a particular energy that we could call the principle of fire, or the Spirit of Fire, or *Ṣango*. This is the *Ifá* view of the multi-level patterns of consciousness in Nature.

Ifá divination is the manipulation of religious symbols as a problem solving process. It is not fortune telling. *Ifá* divination is based on the idea of preserving the wisdom of the past. It is based on the idea that if we do A and B then C will be the result. Most divination systems use transcendent symbols or metaphysical images, in one form or another. These symbols are manipulated to give illumination to a problem or a certain set of circumstances. It is usually believed that Spirit somehow influences the manipulation of the oracle.

Carl Jung did a study of divination systems and invented the word synchronicity to explain why divination works. Jung used the word synchronicity to describe seemingly unrelated events having an underlying meaning. His basis for creating the word synchronicity was the idea that the whole Universe is inter-related, which is consistent with *Ifá* belief. It is the idea that nothing can happen unconnected to anything else. If you are walking down the street and you say; "Should I go right or left? I stubbed my left toe, I should go to the left," you are creating your own communication with the Universe. That is synchronicity based on the psychological model.

Another model, the view of parapsychology is that divination works because the unconscious mind is able to manipulate matter, a phenomenon known as telekinesis.

Ifá considers divination direct communication with Spirit. There are traditionally four ways of communicating with Spirit: divination, possession, the interpretation of dreams and reading signs in Nature. For example, a sudden shift in the weather, or the appearance of something like an epidemic would be considered messages directly from Spirit; consequently they are interpreted as such. Reading signs is sometimes difficult for those of us who live in the city, but it is a significant part of *Ifá* as it is practiced in Africa. Reading signs would include the movement of animals, the movement of birds, following the course of a contagious illness, sudden changes in the weather and so on.

In *Ifá* there is a system of notation used as mandalas, which are symbols of energy patterns. The symbols are based on two figures; a single line I, and a double line II. The anthropologists tend to translate the meaning of this as masculine and feminine. That is way too superficial an analysis. The single line represents the force for expansion in the Universe, and the double line represents the force for contraction in the Universe. They are really understood in Africa as phenomena that predate the emergence of gender. The symbol of expansion and a symbol of contraction that manifest in the physical universe is a single vertical line for light (I) and double vertical lines for darkness (II). There is no connotation of one being better than the other. It is the issue of balancing these two forces that is at the foundation of the spiritual quest.

These marks are grouped together in two pairs of quadragrams, or two pairs of four marks. For example;

```
 I    I
II   II
 I    I
 I   II
```

If you have eight possible marks and two possible marks for each position you have 256 possible combinations. In other words, each place in the eight positions can be either one or two marks. If you count up all the possible combinations it comes to 256.

Each of these markings is called *Odù.* The word *Odù* in Yoruba means womb. Each one of these 256 symbols is believed to be a fundamental energy pattern that sustains Creation on all the different levels of Being. These marks are considered a map of the way that energy can manifest in the world. They are two-dimensional images of a three dimensional reality. *Odù* is not a circle on a mat or tray, the circle represents a sphere. Within the circle there are lines of influence formed by powers of expansion and contraction. If you have a sphere, a gyroscope, and you have forces pulling and pushing, then that is the basic diagram for atomic structure. In traditional Yoruba culture the person who is given credit for working this out is the *Ifá* Prophet *O̲runmila.*

Ifá has 256 *Odù* and each *Odù* represents a particular way that consciousness organizes itself in the Universe. Modern psychology has sixteen character types, based on the polarity between introversion and extroversion. *Ifá* has 256 character types times 12, because each *Odù* can be modified in at least 12 different ways. This means *Ifá* has identified 3072 character types based on this simple scheme.

When these marks are made, in addition to being a mandala, or a blueprint of energy patterns in the Universe, they become a system for organizing data. It is very similar to a computer program that works on the principle of two quadragrams with on/ off switches. It is exactly the same mathematical formation. If each one of these images represents a particular organization of consciousness, then what was done initially was to go through and create scripture that speaks symbolically and poetically about the inner essence of a particular pattern.

If you are learning *Ifá* as a young person in Africa, you first go through the 256 marks and learn the scripture. For example; "Bit by bit we eat the head of the rat, bit by bit we eat the head of the fish, *Ifá* says it is slowly that we progress towards spiritual elevation." This is the first verse of *Ifá*. So you go through and learn the poetic verse. But if you then decide you want to specialize in farming, you go through and relearn all 256 adding the information within your community about farming that relates to each *Odù*. If you were a warrior you would learn the information for each *Odù* that relates to martial arts. *Ifá* has its own martial art called *Aki*. If you were to learn herbal medicine, you would go through and study the verses as they relate to herbs, architecture, or organizing government. It becomes very much like a computer program in the sense that you can have different subjects that plug into the windows on the screen.

Because the information is passed orally, it becomes a way of both making sure you have learned everything because you work your way through the entire system, and it becomes a way of adding new information to any particular subject in the spectrum of the whole system. The marks of *Odù* also become the basis for written language within the culture. The anthropologists say that Africans did not have a written language. Take the mark for the *Odù Odi Ogbe*:

```
I   I
I   II
I   II
I   I
```

Place the mark it on a piece of calabash with charcoal and send it along with a small piece of cloth. This says; "Mother had a baby," and the piece of cloth represents which family she is in. This is written language. You show that to anybody in Yoruba culture and they would read it the same way.

In addition to being a system for organizing the wisdom of the culture, it is a system of communication. It is also a system of invocation, because when you put the mark on the tray and say the prayers that relate to the mark, you bring the Spiritual Forces represented by the pattern to the place where you are doing the divination.

Ifá divination is profoundly complex and not something that you learn overnight. The elders of the village determine who has the aptitude for memorizing certain aspects of the oracle. The selected students usually start their training at seven years old. By the time they are fourteen they have it. This is at least a seven-year process starting at seven and coming to maturity at fourteen. You keep learning for the rest of your life after you have established a solid foundation.

There are several systems that emerge out of the parent system. Most of them are much simpler; to make sure everyone has access to some form of divination or communication with Spirit. Not everyone who worships *Ifá* is going to be able to spend seven years memorizing scripture. For this reason there are simpler systems, all of which are rooted in *Ifá*.

I will start with a simple system and show how it becomes gradually more and more complex. *Ifá* teaches that divination is communication with Spirit. *Ifá* teaches that Spirit will communicate with you using any system you are using, as long as you remain consistent within that system. You can start off learning the system with just a few elements. That would be the same thing as using a Ouji board with only eight letters. You would be limited in the number of words you could use. As you introduce more letters into the system the vocabulary would increase.

In the beginning we work with a system that gives us a yes/no answer to direct questions. Essentially we are working with two words, yes or no. As we develop skill in that system it can give you insights into deeper esoteric levels. Communication with Spirit through divination is not just automatic because you have the cola nuts. The link between the diviner and the Spirit is a consequence of his or her own internal process. In other words you could be an initiated elder and a wise person and have a bad day and you are not making the connection. There are a number of things that are done to insure the link between diviner and Spirit is solid. One of the ways this is done is by casting the oracle in sacred space. By sacred space, I mean an area designated, consecrated and only used for the purpose of divination. The way space is consecrated for divination in *Ifá* is through the use of a mat. The mat is woven; the weave symbolizes the inter-relatedness of all things in Creation. The mat in *Ifá* represents sacred space.

We want to bring the elements of earth, air, fire and water to the sacred space because those are the fundamental elements of Creation. We use a candle, and a glass of water. The earth is there. That may not be literally true if you are sitting on the second floor of an apartment building. But symbolically you are always sitting on the earth. It is considered bad form not to sit on the mat because you want your body touching the earth. You take the candle, the glass of water, the earth and the air we breathe. Now candles are rare and expensive items in Africa. They use palm oil lamps with wool wicks. Sometimes water is not as accessible so these are not hard and fast rules.

In this country, I would suggest that beginning divination be done with four cowries. In Africa they generally use obi kola among many other things. So there is nothing inherently significant about the cowries other than they were used as money and represents abundance. In Africa four cowries are used less than obi. In the Diaspora gluing cowries on pieces of coconut has become popular and this system of divination is generally known in the West as *Obi Abata.*

Once we have earth, air, fire and water on the mat, we want to align with Spirit by what's called *oriki*, the Yoruba word for invocation. We want to invoke that which we are speaking to, or more specifically we want to invite Spirit to the mat. We do not want to just randomly toss the cowries.

It is our belief, and I think out of respect for the ancient history of *Ifá* we should honor the idea, that we only speak to that which we are sanctioned to invoke.

In Africa everyone has sanction to speak to their ancestors. How could you not have that? It is impossible for me to give you that right, and it is impossible for anybody to give you that right. Speaking to your ancestors is a birthright.

The important consideration in speaking to the ancestors is the *Ifá* belief that we become who we are by standing on the shoulders of those who come before us. In other words, every generation does not have to reinvent the wheel. We turn to our ancestors for guidance and we can turn to different ancestors for different issues. Fundamentally we turn to our ancestors for spiritual enlightenment, physical and emotional healing, protection and issues of physical survival. If you have a relative who was a good auto mechanic and your car broke down, you invoke the spirit of that ancestor for guidance. If you are physically ill and you had a relative who was a doctor or a nurse, you might want to talk to them. If you have a relative who was a master at *Aki*, which is *Ogun's* martial art, you may want to invoke that ancestor for protection. If you have questions of how to proceed with what I would call questions of spiritual and ethical concern, it is the grandparent who set a good example we call on.

Ifá is based on the belief that we are all related. We do not have to limit our contact with the ancestors to recent blood relatives. We may have what I call affinity Spirits. Anybody who is a historical figure who has inspired you in any arena is somebody who can guide you.

When you use the mat it is placed on the floor. In Africa it is usually placed on the floor of what is called *Igbodu* from the elision *igbo odu* meaning womb of the forest.

Anyplace you put a pot, or a shrine or something that represents a Force in Nature is called *Igbodu*. It is also a word that is sometimes used to refer to initiation.

The Yoruba word for shrine is *Ojubo*, which means eye your offering, or in better English face your offering. The anthropologists say that the Africans are worshipping fetishes. The elders say the shrine is a place you face when you're saying your prayers. There is no misconception that the rock or the statue is the Spirit. The rock is a receptacle for your prayers, which then becomes a magnet for Forces in Nature that are greater than the rock. The reason I say rock is because most shrines contain a rock in one form or another.

In *Ifá* the elders say when you invoke for divination the *Ifá* diviner returns to the time when *O̱runmila* walked the earth. That is a poetic phrase that refers to a certain alternate form of consciousness in which you are in touch with Spirit, but you are also there in the room, able to speak with the person who is with you. In the south they call this being two headed. It's not full possession, but it is an alternate state of consciousness. It is not something you can just turn on one day and say; "Well time to divine, I guess I'll have to be two headed, I'll flip my two headed switch."

The way you develop spiritual sensitivity is through spiritual discipline. Yoruba culture is based on a four day week and every four days you say prayers to those spirits that you are particularly close to, or that you have been initiated for. In addition to the prayers, you develop what I call your alignment with Spirit. When you are called on to divine, you have been doing the ongoing work of developing a relationship with Spirit every four days. There is a particular sensation that occurs when you are in touch with Spirit. The feeling is very distinct, so you can tell when its there. When you do invocations every four days, when you are starting out you sit there and pray until you feel that. The thing you feel is the thing you felt when you were initiated, so you know what you are looking for. When I was initiated I felt a certain way, four days later I wanted to feel that same way and I wanted to keep praying until I felt that. What you feel is good about yourself. *Ifa* says we are all good and blessed people, we all have the birth right of long life, abundance and good family relationships or children. When you integrate all the various parts of your consciousness, the mind and the body, you do not think negative thoughts about yourself. What comes up is that I am a good and blessed person. When you invoke that, it has a certain feeling, tone, and sensation in your body, which then becomes a magnet for the Spirits you are calling. When you start out sometimes it takes hours of prayer to get to that point. As you progress sometimes you can do it very quickly.

Be clear: none of the *oriki* are etched in stone. There are certain formats that are used to cover certain metaphysical areas that we want to deal with. I want to give you the kind of structure that we deal with because we do not all speak Yoruba. When you are starting out its all right to speak English or whatever language you are comfortable using. Once you see the structure of *oriki* you can effectively use your own language to begin to communicate with the Forces that you are addressing.

If you have completed *oriki* and you still do not feel connected, you do not feel two headed. What do you do next? You have some different options. One of the things you may want to do is *Iba se* your ancestors. *Iba se* means I soul power. Sometimes Yoruba does not translate easily into English. I soul power means I bond, or I connect my spirit to the power of spirit then you call the name of the ancestor. For example; *Iba se* grandfather Fenyes, or in better Yoruba *Iba se Babagba* Fenyes. But you can also say "*Mo juba Babagba* Fenyes, which means I respect grandfather

Fenyes, or if you want to be more formal you can say *Iba se Babagba* Fenyes *mo juba*, or you could say *Iba se Awon ara Orun Ile* Fenyes *mo juba*, which means I praise those members of the Fenyes family who sit at the feet of the Immortals and give them respect. You want to be colorful and descriptive when you are saying invocations and you want to put some feeling into it.

At this point, if you still do not feel connected you can sing. For example *a iba se, iba se o, iba baba, iba yeye iba se o*. It is all right to sing at this point. Its all right to tell the ancestors what it is you are doing, why you are calling them. We do that by identifying our self. In Yoruba *emi* means I am. I would say *Emi Awo* Falokun Fatunmbi *fun mi ire* meaning I am Awo Falokun Fatunmbi asking for your blessing. If you are just starting, it is all right to speak in English and say Ancestors I am *Awo* Falokun, I am here asking for your blessing. Sit quietly and ask the ancestors questions as if you are talking to a living person. Allow yourself to feel the response. When you get an impression, check the impression with divination. At this point all you want is a yes/no answer. Keep it simple, four shells up and two shells up are yes answers, everything else is a no. As you become adept at this process, some of the no answers become a maybe. At this point the maybe answers should be considered a no. You want to develop an understanding of when the ancestors are speaking with you and by keeping the divination process simple you can concentrate on your main objective.

To move beyond the yes/no answers of divination requires an understanding of mandalas. A mandala is a map of consciousness. Every spiritual tradition I am aware of has some form of mandala art, for example Navajo sand paintings, and Tibetan Buddhism uses mandalas in their temple art. A mandala is any symbolic picture sectioned into four quadrants. Each quadrant represents a different aspect of consciousness. The mandala usually becomes the focal point of meditation. Mandala art is also the basis for most sacred architecture. The Egyptians made use of the mandala idea as the basis for building their temples. The entire ascetic of Islam religious art is rooted in this concept. Islam does not make representations of the physical features of prophetic leaders, so the artwork on the walls of Mosques is a geometric expression of metaphysical concepts making extensive use of mandala patterns.

In *Ifá* we have the image of the endless weave, a pattern that is sown into the clothing of *Ifá* diviners. When you see someone in Africa with this design on their robe or on their hat, you know they are a diviner. The symbolic meaning of the endless weave suggests everything is interconnected.

There are a number of implements that are used for divination. Coconut is used throughout the Diaspora. I prefer using cowry shells. The shells have one side that looks like a mouth and another side that has a hump on it. When these shells are used for divination the hump is poked out. This reveals a little bar that runs across the inside of the shell; this side is called the stomach. Every shell used in divination has a mouth and a stomach. The mouth represents the force of expansion and the stomach represents the force of contraction. Words expand by going out of the mouth and into the universe. Food is contracted and reconstituted within the stomach. When you contract something it eventually reduces to darkness, the idea of the black hole. When you expand something it creates electromagnetic radiation, which is the source of light. We have two polarities: light and dark. Neither one is good or bad; there is no pejorative connotation of one being better than the other. Whenever you have a polarity it always means that the two components are equal.

The concept of darkness and the concept of light are related to two principles of consciousness. Light is related to the concept of *ori ire*. *Ori* is the Yoruba word for consciousness or inner spirit. The word is sometimes used to mean head, but the inference is always consciousness. In *Ifá* consciousness includes all the neurological, psychic and unconscious input that forms individual identity. *Ori ire* means consciousness of good fortune.

Ifá teaches reincarnation, so it is our belief that everybody has a destiny they have chosen before coming to this lifetime. If you are living the destiny you have chosen you will receive the blessings of abundance, long life and family. When you are in alignment with your destiny you are said to be moving along the path of light, you are in pursuit of *ori ire*. In this context *ori ire* would mean wisdom.

Ori ibi is the consciousness of darkness or contraction. Again this is not bad. The word *ibi* in Yoruba means afterbirth. When a baby is born the placenta was the source of life for the baby in the womb. Once the baby comes out of the womb the umbilical cord must be cut or the baby will die. *Ori ibi* suggests that in order to move along your path of destiny something needs to be discarded. The obvious example would be insecurity. The person who applies for a job by saying; "I think I can do it, but I'm not sure." Clearly, this person needs to let go of the sense of self-doubt because it becomes a form of symbolic afterbirth, something that needs to be discarded.

If there is an issue of *ibi* when you are doing divination, it means that there is something that needs to be let go of. In the example I have given, the *ibi* would be insecurity. The question then becomes: how do we determine what is in alignment with our destiny and what needs to be discarded. That is the fundamental issue in any form of *Ifá* divination. When you understand the metaphysical foundation of the yes/no divination process there is a wealth of information at your disposal.

What I want to suggest is that this system is like an unfolding flower with layers and layers of profound depth in regard to exploring the potential for communication with Spirit, you can become as sophisticated, as probing, and as studious as you want. You could spend a lifetime studying the use of four cowries and know you still have more to learn.

Not everyone is going to become an expert in divination, but it is my belief that if you say the invocations, and if your heart is in a good place, Spirit will speak to you at the level of the oracle you are using. If all you can do is speak in terms of yes and no, then Spirit will speak to you on that basis. If you have more options, Spirit will speak to you taking advantage of other options. It will do so in order to fine-tune the clarity of the message.

The mandala used in *Ifá* is a circle with an equal armed cross. This image is a map of *ori*. We have the cross marking the four directions of the compass. The left side of the horizontal line of the cross represents the past. The right side of the horizontal line of the cross represents the future. The top portion of the vertical line of the cross represents spiritual influences. The bottom portion of the vertical line of the cross represents survival influences.

In brief terms, the spirits who preserve the past are ancestors or *Egun*. The spirits who bring in the future are called *Ibamole*, which means Spirits of the House of Light. These spirits are sometimes called *Igbamole*, which means Spirits of the Calabash of Light. These are variations in dialect, but they both have the same function—to bring in the future. Spiritual influences come from *Orişa*. Survival influences come from *Ogboni* and *Irunmole*. *Ogboni* means Wisdom of the Earth. *Irunmole* means House of Light in the Earth.

It is *Ifá's* belief that if we are on our path of destiny, our consciousness is perfectly balanced in all four of these quadrants. The condition of being in alignment with destiny involves discovering the inner self, which is symbolized by the center point of the cross on the tray; the place where the two lines intersect. It is our belief, and my experience that if you balance all of these factors, if you are sitting quietly, you can find the inner self. If you are sitting quietly and all of those things are balanced you should experience joy because we believe life is benevolent. If you experience anything other than joy it is an indicator that something is out of balance. It is a really simple test. It is a test in every earth-centered tradition that I am aware of. People judge the wisdom of the elders by how quietly they can sit.

What happens is we get off center and think we are in the center. There are lots of ways that we do this. I will give a few examples of the most obvious ways that we get off center in each of the quadrants. There are people who get stuck in the past. Somebody has a problem in their childhood and everything that happens to them everyday is affected by that event. People who are stuck in the future believe their life will be better just as soon as they get a promotion at work. Some people are obsessed with Survival issues, the need for physical and financial security; they need to make sure the rent is paid on time. People stuck in the spiritual quadrant have what I call the "holier than thou syndrome." They believe everything they do is in alignment with the will of God. In Yoruba culture this is known as arrogance.

If we take the idea that we have four cowries shells and we drop them on a mat, each shell will fall somewhere in these four quadrants. The location of the shells within a particular quadrant can be read as commentary on the fundamental yes/no response. If a shell is mouth up in a particular quadrant, it means the person is in alignment with their destiny in that particular arena. If the shell is face down in a particular quadrant it means that something needs to be let go of in that particular arena. There are no strict rules for evaluating this information. The evaluation must always be done in the context of the overall question. What happens when you start using this process is that the mandala has a triggering effect. That means seeing the issue represented on a two-dimensional plane can stimulate mental associations that reveal deeper levels of perception. The development of this skill comes with practice so in the beginning stages it is important to trust the information that comes up. Make a note of it, then in the future make a very objective evaluation of its accuracy.

The Global Village

The Ifá Concept of Oba Igbaye

MY GRANDFATHER ADELBURT FENYES crossed over many years before I was born. In 1969 for a brief instant I saw his image in a mirror. After the impression faded I saw a line of ghostly apparitions standing in the room. Overwhelmed I laid down on the couch and had an out of body experience. My subjective understanding of the strange events that occurred that night was a message from my grandfather telling me to travel to Africa so I could learn something about my ancestors. My grandfather was from Transylvania. At the time the message made no sense. I did my best to ignore it.

Twenty years later I traveled to Ode Remo and was blessed to receive initiation into *E̱gbe̱ Ifá,* Ogunti Ode Remo, the society of diviners in the city of Ode Remo, Ogun State, Nigeria. On my first trip to Africa I had some concerns my ancestral heritage would be an obstacle to initiation and I was fully prepared to study whatever the good people of Ode Remo wanted to share and teach without expectations. The decision to initiate me was based on divination. The *Araba* cast the oracle four times to determine whether or not to proceed with the ritual. The *Odu* that appeared on that day were *Eji Ogbe, Eji Ogbe, Eji Ogbe* and *Odi Meji.* The first three *Odu* were the same, *Eji Ogbe* speaks of perfect alignment with your destiny a clear yes answer to my question. *Odi Meji* speaks of rebirth, the metaphysical principle that supports initiation. Preparations for *tefá* started as soon as the divination was finished.

On the seventh and final day of my elevation the elders of *Ifá* did divination they call *etutu.* The first words spoken by the *Araba* of Ode Remo were, "Take an offering to the home of your grandfather and thank him for bringing you here." I had said nothing to anyone about the odd experience of seeing my grandfather in the mirror. The statement by the *Araba* astonished me and gave me a real sense of the power of *awo.* It also inspired an ancestral quest that has radically altered my sense of self and world.

Transylvania is associated in the minds of the public with Vampires, Count Dracula and the abominations of Dr. Frankenstein. Africa spirituality is associated with Voodoo dolls, hexing and devil worship. In my opinion the denigration of both of these traditions is not accidental or arbitrary.

Transylvania is an anomaly that historians and archeologists prefer to ignore. According to academia written language in Europe emerged 5,000 years ago. There are examples of writing in Transylvania that date back 10,000 years. Recently a topographical map of the region made from porcelain was discovered and dated at 20,000 years old. The map is geographically accurate and shows no signs of weathering or decay. For mainstream academicians these are serious problems because they do not fit the accepted version of history.

What is the explanation for these anomalies? The indigenous people in what is now called Transylvania say they migrated to Eastern Europe from Egypt. The Transylvania Creation Myth speaks of a hunter who followed an antelope from the Nile peninsula to the mountains surrounding the Black Sea. With the discovery of tin, copper and gold Transylvania became a mining colony for the rulers of Egypt, Mesopotamia and may well be the location of the lost mines of King Solomon. If anyone is skeptical of these claim look at photographs of the stone pyramids built in the Crimea and compare them with the pictures of the pyramids in Giza. Not only is the masonry the same, but the astrological alignment is identical as are the angles and geometric proportions. Academia likes to call this a coincidence. I call it cross cultural interaction.

I would suggest to the serious student of African religions that the spirituality of Transylvania is denigrated by the mass media for the same reasons the spirituality of Africa is denigrated by the mass media. Both traditions are linked and both traditions preserve a number of secrets that those who control the global economy want suppressed.

My ancestral name is Fenyes which in Hungarian means bringer of light. The origins of the name are associated with the ancient Transylvanian priesthood, those who preserved the secrets of alchemy, building stone monuments and the sacred ritual of anointing the king. All of these traditions were brought to Eastern Europe many years ago from Africa and remnants of these mysteries have been preserved by the Fenyes clan for many generations. Our emblem is the winged dragon, a symbol used by African initiates who traveled all over the world teaching science, cultural and sacred technology. The European myths associated with slaying the dragon are stories about the political effort to destroy all traces of the ancient wisdom.

The first significant attempt to culturally appropriate the sacred technology of African was the conquest of Alexander the Great who went on an eight year quest to gather the secrets of pre-diluvium culture that existed in the known world. He deposited written records of the wisdom of the Mediterranean, northern Africa, the Middle East and Asia in the great library of Alexandria near the mouth of the Nile. There is evidence to suggest that his search for ancient wisdom was inspired by his teacher Aristotle who was an initiate of the Greek Mystery schools which in turn were associated with the mysteries schools of northern Africa.

Alexander-s legacy was appropriated by the Roman Empire who brought the important books from Alexandria to Italy before burning the library to the ground. Some of the science preserved in Alexandria was rescued by the Egyptian priesthood, taken to Jerusalem and later hidden in the caves under Solomon's temple.

Following the destruction of Israel by the Romans in 70 AD, a large segment of the Jewish Diaspora settled in the region between Southern Spain and Southern France in a country then known as Septmania. They took with them the location of the secret burial places of the ancient wisdom from African that remained hidden in the Middle East.

In the thirteenth century the Knights Templars spent nine years in Jerusalem excavating Solomon's temple. It is not known exactly what they discovered but they did bring highly technical information to France and eventually Scotland that was clearly of African origin. This legacy became the foundation of what is known as the Renaissance. The keepers of this wisdom included men like Leonardo

DeVinci who was not so much an inventor as he was an interpreter of ancient manuscripts.

Following the recovery of documents from Jerusalem, the Knights Templars built over one hundred Gothic Cathedrals using information based on the sacred geometry and architecture of ancient Egypt. In an effort to control the appropriated technology the King of France banned the Knights Templars only to discover their vast library disappeared from Europe. After being declared a heresy many of the members of the Knights Templars fled Europe and were given sanctuary in Scotland and Ethiopia.

Napoleon believed he could reclaim the legacy of the Templars by capturing the library at the Vatican and by colonizing Egypt. Scientist working for Napoleon discovered the Rosetta stone which was the basis for translating Egyptian Hieroglyphics into European languages. The information recovered by Napoleon eventually ended up in the hands of the Hapsburgs, the Royal family of Austria and Hungry. Word War I started following the assassination of Arch Duke Ferdinand in an effort to destroy the Hapsburg lineage and suppress the secret wisdom under their protection. World War II started when Hitler invaded Austria and stole the regalia and the library of the Hapsburgs in Vienna. The legacy stolen by the Nazi's was not returned to Austria instead it became part of the spoils of war and ended up in the hands of American and Russian military intelligence.

This is a different view of history than the one we are accustomed to reading in high school and college text books. It begs the question what was so important that political despots over the ages were willing to wage war in an effort to take possession of the secret wisdom of ancient Africa.

On my second trip to Nigeria I was taken to the *Oni's* palace in Ile Ifẹ. The *Oni* is the senior *Oba* or King of traditional Yoruba culture. While at the palace I met the *Emese,* sixteen *awo* who live behind the *Oni's* residence. Two hundred and sixty-four days a year, with one day off each year, the *Emese* pray for the well being of the Yoruba Nation. They project their prayers on to a stone, which in turn projects the prayers into an underground water system that carries the prayers to the four corners of the northwestern African rain forest. Similarly the entire country of Egypt is supported by a huge underground man made water system which Academic historians refuse to talk about because they cannot grasp the purpose of such a monumental construction project. Identical artificial water systems can be found in most of South America.

The great stone monuments of Europe are built on top of naturally occurring water systems. It was the task of the ancient priesthood to use the stones and water to insure fertility, to maintain peace and establish gateways into the realm of spirit. This technology worked, it was effective, and it was based on a real understanding of the multi-dimensional Universe we all live in. This wisdom is preserved in the myths associated with the search for the Holy Grail.

Alexander the Great was the first to gather the written specifications of this system in one place. The data associated with this astonishing accomplishment has changed hands over the years but is now clearly in the hands of military intelligence where it is used to support the aspirations of those who control the global economy. Confirmation of this comes from the research of Bruce Cathie (*The Energy Grid, Harmonic 695, The Pulse of the Universe*, Adventures Unlimited Press) who has traced the most of the global sacred sites located on the global grid and has discovered unexplained electronic devices at many of these sites. Could this be another coincidence? Cathie does not think so, I don't either.

Ancient Egypt discovered the secret of alchemy. The popular notion is that alchemy is the ability to transform lead into gold and that it is a mythic art taking place in fairy tales along with unicorns, elves, and magic carpets. The science of Alchemy was discovered, or possibly rediscovered during the time of Akhenaton. During his reign the priests of Egypt built huge furnaces at the base of Mt. Sinai. These furnaces were used to smelt iridium which is the secret ingredient in the Alchemical process. The gold produced in Egypt after Akhenaton is largely synthetic and was applied to statues and tombs through the use of electrolysis. At the very least this is indicative of sophisticated metallurgical skills.

When iridium is processed under extreme heat it transforms into a white powder called *mfkzt* by the ancient Egyptians. The secret of *mfkzt* was preserved by the royal families of Transylvania and was accidentally discovered in the early nineteen eighties by an Arizona cotton farmer named David Hudson. He was having trouble farming because of the high sodium content in the black dirt on his land. Egypt was original known as Khemet meaning black earth. The word alchemy is a derivation of Alkhemet meaning light of the black earth. In his effort to analyze the soil, Hudson discovered usually large amounts of iridium which is a derivative of platinum. Under high temperatures iridium looses 56% of its original weight. When it cools the lost weight reappears. This is in contradiction to all accepted laws of physics. The explanation is simple. The structure of iridium makes it an inter-dimensional portal. In the words of *Ifá* iridium in its powdered form is *Odù.* Iridium powder is a super conductor that generates a Meissner field. In the world of quantum physics a Meissner field is used to describe any energy source that is anti-gravitational. This means that placing a line of iridium powder on a large sandstone block makes it weightless. Alchemy is the secret of the construction of the pyramids.

Iridium is a superconductor meaning it is able to draw light from natural magnetic fields. As a fuel source for batteries it has unlimited potential. You could use a single battery with iridium as the active ingredient to run a car for years. This would end the fuel driven energy crisis overnight.

David Hudson built a huge factor to produce iridium for batteries. The factory was the target of arson. FEMA will not allow Hudson to reopen his plant. The price of oil continues to go up, while a small group of people continue to increase their wealth.

Powdered iridium can also be used as medicine. Ingested the super conductor quality of iridium can regenerate the tips of DNA molecules. The degeneration of the ends of a DNA strand is the source of both aging and the destruction of the immune system. The FDA refuses to give permission for anyone to study the use of iridium as a cure for AIDS or cancer. The refusal comes without explanation. If iridium does not work what is the harm in conducting research?

The use of iridium as medicine has a positive side effect. It opens the powers of human perception and allows individuals to see the otherwise invisible dimensions of reality on the upper and lower ends of the light spectrum.

In ancient times iridium was used in conjunction with star fire oil to anoint the Pharaohs and later the kings of the Pharaonic dynasty. Star fire oil is a mixture of human menstrual blood and crocodile fat. When this oil is rubbed on the forehead it opens the pituitary gland and facilities the ability to astral travel. The ability to astral travel is the ability to separate your consciousness from physical body. It is the ability to see anything, anywhere at anytime in the past or the future. During the cold war military intelligence, the CIA and the FBI developed and used a system for teaching astral travel to their agents, calling it remote viewing. The tactic used by those who have access to this technology is to keep the information from the public as part of an ongoing policy of divide and conquer. This policy puts nations at war, while those who profit from the tools of war accumulate huge personal fortunes.

In 1920 Rwanda was given to the Belgians at a conference in Berlin called to create arbitrary boundaries needed to divide the spoils of colonialism in Africa. When the Belgians arrived they were horrified to discover the region had only one culture, one language and one history. The Belgians made the decision to call everyone who lived in the country a Hutu and everyone who lived in the city a Tutsi. They issued identity cards so everyone would know which group they belonged to. The colonialists systematically executed the local religious elders and imposed Catholicism as the state religion of the region. They trained the Tutsis for political power and deliberately fostered jealousy and cultural animosity as a method of maintaining political control. Eighty years later this policy led to mass genocide followed by a media campaign designed to place all the blame for this tragedy on the Africans.

This is but one of many examples of the policy of divide and conquer used to shape consciousness for political and economic goals that benefit the few at the expense of the many. We live in a consensus reality which means our perception of the world around us is shaped by collective agreement. Whenever I tell anyone I am Transylvanian the consensus reality conjures images of blood suckers, monsters and demons that shape shift into bats at night. Virtually no one associates the legacy of Transylvania with the secrets of Alchemy and the lost technology used in the stone temples that cover the surface of the earth. My point is this negative association is deliberate. Cultures have been conditioned in ways that have nothing to do with the real history and the accomplishments of any given part of the world. In simple terms the planet is suffering from deliberately generated bias. For most of my life Americans were conditioned to hate and fear communists, especially those who lived in Russia. One day the Berlin Wall fell and communism was official over. In a relatively short time the evil other became described as a Muslim Fundamentalist. This is an unending cycle of manipulation and control that is contrary to the *Ifá* view of good character and family responsibility.

The prejudices that shape our perceptions tend to become ancestral, inherited from past generations and passed onto future descendants. If we want to create extended family based on the *Ifá* model we need to examine the ideas that shape our perceptions of each other and determine if they have any basis in fact. One of the ways this can be done is through communal *egun* ritual.

Spiritual growth involves finding our personal center and placing that in correct relationship with our family, our community and our planet. The science of genetics says everyone alive on the earth today is the descendant of a single East African woman. *Ifá* says everyone alive today has common ancestral spirit called *Oba Igbaye.* There is no scientific or metaphysical basis for excluding anyone from the global village.

In America people have come from all over the world. In addition to the deep wounds caused by slavery, there are ethnic tensions from countless decades of war, exploitation, genocide and unrestrained racism in many forms. If these wounds are addressed one at a time through the intervention of ancestral spirits they can be transformed at their source. This type of work requires trust and a sincere desire to resolve old conflicts. There is also the danger that efforts to heal old wounds will make them worse. Avoiding the risk insures failure. The path of elevatoin and healing ivolves embracing all the dimensions of our collective family spirit.

Lesson 6

Making an Ancestor Pot Divination

PART 2

AWẸ́ OBÌ ÀBÀTÀ

(Segments of the kola nut used in divination)

Obì àbàtà is a kola nut (*cola acuminata sterculiaceare*) used in African forms of *Ifá/Òrìṣà* worship as an implement for divination. In some regions of Nigeria it is referred to as *obì gidi*. It is a small red nut with two to four segments called *awẹ́*. The segments generally have two distinct shapes identified as masculine (*ọkunrin*) and feminine (*obinrin*). Masculine segments are narrow and appear phallic. Feminine segments are wider and appear uterine. Each segment has a top and a bottom. The top is the section closest to the stem of the nut. For purposes of identification the top is the section furthest away from the seed pod.

OBÌ ÀBÀTÀ AWẸ ẸNU ATI INÙ

(The mouth and the stomach of the kola nut segments)

Each segment of *obì àbàtà* has a mouth and a stomach. The mouth is the side of the nut that is exposed when it is open and the stomach is the side of the segment that is exposed when it is closed. The mouth could be described as the inside of the nut and the stomach could be described as the outside or the skin of the nut.

OBÌ ÀBÀTÀ AWẸ MÉJÌ

(Kola nut divination using two segments)

Using a nut with two segments the combinations of throws are as follows:

1. One male segment mouth up = *Ìlera* = yes with a blessing of stability.
2. One female segment mouth up = *Ajé* = yes with a blessing of wealth.
3. One male segment up, one female segment up = *Alàáfia* = yes with a blessing of an open road.

Both segments with the mouth down = *Ọyẹkú* = no.

This system is most often used during the course of an elaborate ritual when food offerings (*adimu*) are made. *Obí àbàtà* is used for divination and functions as a common form or food offering accepted by most *Òrìṣà* as *adimu*. The word *adimu* refers to any offering that does not involve slaughtering an animal for food.

ADIMU IS̱OTÉ̱LÈ

(Food as segments of Divination)

Whenever food such as yam or apples is given as *adimu* offerings to Spirit it is possible to cut slices of these foods so they have a mouth and a stomach. The mouth is the internal surface and the stomach is the external surface. When this is done the process may involve the use of two implements that have no masculine or feminine characteristics. In this instance the combinations of throws are as follows:

1. One mouth up = *Ejire* = yes with a blessing from Spirit.
2. Two mouths up = *Alàáfia* = yes with a blessing of an open road.

Two mouths down = *oyeku* = no

OBÌ ÀBÀTÀ AWÉ̱ ME̱RIN

(Kola nut divination using four segments)

The most common method of divination in African forms of *Odù Ifá/Òrìs̱à* worship is the use of *obí àbàtà* with four segments. This type of divination is used both to check on the progress of a ritual and as a way of accessing *Odu Ifa*. This system is multi-dimensional and can be approached in a number of different ways. The most direct method involves yes no answers to a formulated question. The questions should be simple and direct. They should be constructed so the desired result comes with a yes answer. In other words it is better to ask the question will I receive abundance than to ask the question will I always be poor. The positive answer to the first questions is yes, the positive answer to the second question is no.

The combinations of yes/no answers using four segments of *obí àbàtà* are as follows:

1. One male segment mouth up = *Ìlera* = yes with a blessing of stability or a blessing of triumph over difficulty depending on the nature of the question.
2. One female segment mouth up = *Ajé* = yes with a blessing of abundance or wealth depending on the nature of the question. (In *Odù Ifá* abundance includes wealth, long life and children.)
3. One male segment mouth up and one female segment mouth up = *Ejire* = yes with a blessing from Spirit. (*Ejire* represents balance, and this suggests coolness or friendliness depending on the nature of the question.)
4. Two male segments mouth up = *Akonran* = no with a struggle of hardship or quarrel depending on the nature of the question.
5. Two female segments mouth up = *Ero* = yes with a blessing of calmness, or rest after struggle depending on the nature of the question.
6. Two male segments mouth up and one female segment mouth up = *Akita* = yes with a blessing of success after some difficulty. (This combination suggests a need for will and determination to gain the desired result, which means the outcome may be in doubt.)
7. Two female segments mouth up and one male segment mouth up = *Obita* = yes with a blessing

of manifestation with little or no effort, a blessing of peace and an end to quarrel depending on the nature of the question.

8. Two male segments mouth up and two female segments mouth up = *Alàáfia* = yes with a blessing of an open road.
9. All segments mouth down = *O̱ye̱kú* = no.

OBÌ ÀBÀTÀ ODÙ

(Translation of kola nut divination into *Odù*)

The system of *obí àbàtà* may be used in a simple yes/no context or it may be used as a reference to *Odù*. There are several systems for making reference to *Odù*. Each system is based on a regional variation of the process and no system is inherently better than another. If you have elders follow the system of their lineage. If you have no teachers decide which system will be used and then use that system consistently. Spirit will speak to the diviner using whatever system is in place. If the diviner changes systems in hopes of getting a more favorable answer the result is confusion.

The most common method of transferring *obì àbàtà* into *Odù* is to read the pieces from the top of the tray down and to translate each segment into either a single line (I) or a double line (II). The side of the kola nut with a skin on it is read as a double line and the inner surface of the kola nut is read as a single line.

When asking a yes/no question the *Odù* that is formed by the segments can be used as commentary on the yes/no response. A single throw forms 1/2 a leg of *Odù Ifá*. The patterns of *Odù Ifá* are made up of two quadrams that form a single octogram. Each quadragram is called a leg of *Ifá* and two quadragrams form a complete *Odù*. In order to read four segments of *obì àbàtà* as *Odù Ifá* the quadragram is doubled so that both legs of the pattern are identical. There are 16 *Odù* in the *Ifá* system that have identical legs on both sides of the octogram. These *Odù* are called méjì which means *twice* in Yoruba. The 16 *méjì Odù* are called *Olodù* which means Spirit of the *Odù*. The *Olodù* appear as follows:

I I
I I
I I
I I

Ogbe Méjì

II II
II II
II II
II II

Oyeku

II II
I I
I I
II II

MéjìIwori Méjì

I I
II II
II II
I I

Odi Méjì

I I
I I
II II
II II

Irosun Méjì

II II
II II
I I
I I

Oworin Méjì

I I
II II
II II
II II

Obara Méjì

II II
II II
II II
I I

Okanran Méjì

I I I I I I II II	II II I I I I I I
Ogunda Méjì	***O̱sa Méjì***
II II I I II II II II	II II II II I I II II
Ika Méjì	***Oturupon Méjì***
I I II II I I I I	I I I I II II I I
Otura Méjì	***Ire̱te̱ Méjì***
I I II II I I II II	II II I I II II I I
O̱se̱ Méjì	***Ofun Méjì***

When the transposition from quadragram to octogram is made the verses and the metaphysical principles related to each of the *méjì Odù* may be considered as part of the response to the question. For those diviners who know the divination system of *Mérìndinlogun* (16 cowries), the *Méjì* may be transposed into *Odù Mérìndinlogun* as follows:

1.	*Ogbe Méjì*	=	*Eji Ogbe*
2.	*Oyeku Méjì*	=	*Eji Òko*
3.	*Iwori Méjì*	=	*Ejila Sebora*
4.	*Odi Méjì*	=	*Odi*
5.	*Irosun Méjì*	=	*Irosun*
6.	*Owonrin Méjì*	=	*Owonrin*
7.	*Obara Méjì*	=	*Obara*
8.	*Okanran Méjì*	=	*Okanran*
9.	*Ogunda Méjì*	=	*Ogunda*
10.	*Osa Méjì*	=	*Osa*
11.	*Ika Méjì*	=	*Ika*
12.	*Oturupon Méjì*	=	*Oturupon*
13.	*Otura Méjì*	=	*Ofun Kanran*
14.	*Irete Méjì*	=	*Irete*
15.	*Ose Méjì*	=	*Ose*
16.	*Ofun Méjì*	=	*Ofun*

Those diviners who are familiar with *Mérìndinlogun* may use *obì àbàtà* instead of 16 cowries as tools of divination. Instead of asking a yes/no question, the diviner simply asks for an *Odù* that will illuminate a particular problem. The advantage of using *obì àbàtà* is that it is possible to throw *obì àbàtà* without the obligation to make *ebo* (offerings). Using *obì àbàtà* would then be used to clarify simple matters while *Mérìndinlogun* would be used to address spiritual matters that require personal transformation and ritual support.

Those diviners who are familiar with *Ifá* may use *obì àbàtà* instead of *o̱pe̱le̱* or *ikin* as tools of divination. Instead of asking a yes/no question, the diviner again simply asks for an *Odù* that will illuminate a particular problem. When using *obì àbàtà* for *Ifá* divination, the diviner may either throw once to receive an *Odù Méjì* or throw twice to receive any of the 256 *Odù* in the complete corpus of *Odù*. When two throws are used to get two different legs (quadragrams) of *Ifá*, the first throw is the right leg and the second throw is the left leg.

IRE/IBI

(Determining orientation of the *Odù*)

The system of divination based on *obì àbàtà* has several methods for the determination of the orientation of the *Odù*. Orientation means the *Odù* comes with *ire*, which means good fortune or *ibi* which means obstacles to good fortune. In the systems of *Mé̱rìndinlogun* and *Ifá* the method for determining orientation involves additional throws. To determine orientation in *obì àbàtà* no additional throw is required. Instead an examination of the kola segments reveals the orientation. Each segment has both a top and a bottom. The top of the segment is the section closest to the stem. The top is also the section furthest away from the seedpod. The orientation of the *Odù* is determined either by using the segment closest to the top of the tray, or by using the segment with the mouth up that is closest to the top of the tray. Either method may be used as long as it is consistent. In both systems the orientation is as follows:

1. Male segment top facing the top of the tray = *ire*.
2. Male segment top facing the bottom of the tray = *ibi*.
3. Female segment top facing the top of the tray = *ibi*.
4. Female segment top facing the bottom of the tray = *ire*.

I recommend that the student who is new to divination begin the study process with just the yes/no elements then add levels, as each new component is fully understood.

In the Diaspora there is extensive attention to the issue of orientation and where the *ire* or *ibi* comes from. In my lineage there is a belief that all divination needs to end in *ire* and it is the job of the diviner to find it. *Ibi* is essential resistance to the lessons of *Odu* and resistance is ultimately rooted in *ori* or consciousness. If a person does not embrace a lesson brought by Spirit and does not use that lesson as a basis for personal growth, the lesson is destined to return. In many ways divination is a system designed to avoid the frustration and disappointment of making the same mistakes over and over again.

When we say we stand on the shoulders of those who have come before us we are saying we are committed to the process of learning a better way based on our willingness to avoid the problems of the past. It is our ancestors who bring us a clear vision of a better way.

Appendix

Yoruba Pronunciation

THERE ARE TWENTY-FIVE LETTERS in the Yoruba language, seven vowels and eighteen consonants.

The vowels are A E E̲ I O O̲ U. The marks under the letters E̲ and O̲ create different sounds from the letters E and O, without the marks. Any mark under a Yoruba means you add an H sound to the letter. Marks are found under E, O and S.

The Yoruba alphabet with English words that have the same sound or intonations.

A (ah)	Sounds like the A in Ark
B (bee)	Sounds like the B in Bee
D (dee)	Sounds like the D in Deal

E (ay) — Sounds like the E in Eight

E (eh) — Sounds like the E in Egg

F (fee) — Sounds like the F in Feel

G (gi) — Sounds like the G in Give

GB — No English equivalent

H (hee) — Sounds like the H in Hill

I (ee) — Sounds like the I in Bee

J (gee) — Sounds like the J in Jeep

K (kee) — Sounds like the K in Keep

L (lee) — Sounds like the L in Leaf

M (mee) — Sounds like the M in Milk

N (nee) — Sounds like the N in Nil

O (aw) — Sounds like the O in Odd

O (oh) — Sounds like the O in Oh

P (pi) — Sounds like the P in Pit

R (ree) — Sounds like the R in Read

S (cee) — Sounds like the S in Sea

S (Sh) — Sounds like the S in Sheep

T (tee) — Sounds like the T in Tea

U (oo) — Sounds like the U in You

W (we) — Sounds like the W in We

Y (yee) — Sounds like the Y in Yield

Yoruba language is tonal meaning the relative pitch of letters effects the meaning of the word. There are three basic tones used in Yoruba that be described as *do re mi* or the first three notes of the tempered scale. Normal speaking voice would be *re,* an accent slanting from left to right would be *mi,* and an accent slanting from right to left is *do.*